The Polymer Clay Cookbook

THE

Polymer Clay
COOKBOOK

···

TINY FOOD JEWELRY TO WHIP UP AND WEAR

···

Jessica Partain and Susan Partain

WATSON-GUPTILL PUBLICATIONS / NEW YORK

Dedication

To our parents, who have always been incredibly supportive of all of our creative endeavors

Design by Jess Morphew
Cover photography © 2009 by Zachary Williams
Text copyright © 2009 by Jessica and Susan Partain
Styled project photography copyright © 2009 by Zachary Williams
How-to photography copyright © 2009 by Jessica and Susan Partain

First published in the United States in 2009 by
Watson-Guptill Publications, an imprint of the Crown
Publishing Group, a division of Random House, Inc.,
1745 Broadway, New York, NY 10019
www.crownpublishing.com
www.watsonguptill.com

WATSON-GUPTILL is a registered trademark and the WG
and Horse designs are trademarks of Random House, Inc.

Library of Congress Cataloging-in-Publication Data
Partain, Jessica.
  The polymer clay cookbook : tiny food jewelry to whip up and wear /
Jessica and Susan Partain.
     p. cm.
  ISBN 978-0-8230-2484-1 (alk. paper)
  1. Polymer clay craft. 2. Jewelry making. 3. Food in art.
  4. Cookery.
I. Partain, Susan. II. Title.
  TT297.P265 2009
  745.594'2—dc22

                              2009015971

Printed in China

First printing, 2009

1 2 3 4 5 6 7 8 / 15 14 13 12 11 10 09

Acknowledgments

We couldn't have done this without the help of many other people! First and foremost we'd like to thank our parents for their constant encouragement and for buying us those first packets of polymer clay when we were kids. We also owe thanks to the rest of our family, who taught us to celebrate and enjoy all varieties of food. To Stephanie Andregg-Maloy, everyone at the Charlottesville City Market, and all of our awesome customers who help to make Inedible Jewelry a success.

JESSICA ✳ I would also especially like to thank Barbara Kreuter for her enthusiastic support and help reading a huge chunk of the manuscript, and all of the students from the Staunton Library and the Jefferson-Madison Regional Library classes for their exuberance and fantastic questions. I'd also like to thank everyone from the Sunday night dinner crowd for being amazing real cooks, and for your well-timed pints of ice cream (Jackie), fresh cobbler (Angie), hummus (Steven), guacamole (Chris), and shrimp (Hugh).

SUSAN ✳ Special thanks to Brent for the patience, the countless meals provided, and the seemingly unlimited use of his laptop.

And finally, we'd like to thank Julie Mazur, Cathy Hennessy, and all the lovely people at Watson-Guptill who made this book a reality.

Contents

Introduction

Why We're Obsessed with Tiny Food Jewelry
(and Why You Should Be, Too!)

As sisters, we first discovered polymer clay as kids, and haven't been able to put it down since. Combine our love of clay with a healthy obsession with food, and naturally we pour our creativity into cooking up miniature polymer clay food jewelry. We love thinking about our favorite foods and how to replicate them as realistic miniatures. Most of all, we love sharing our passion for food, and watching people dangle a cupcake around their neck—or waffles from their ears!

Food isn't just about the taste—it's about memories, emotions, and people. We all have favorite foods that evoke ties to special times and places in our lives. Who can eat watermelon without remembering twilight summer picnics? Or pretzels without thinking about long afternoons at the ballpark? We particularly love gingerbread cookies, not only because of their delicious flavor, but because they bring us back to childhood days spent carefully decorating each one to look like a member of our family. To celebrate food is, we think, to celebrate life.

We've designed this book as a "cookbook" for the beginning miniature "chef," and just like a regular cookbook, we begin with the basics. The main "ingredient" of our food miniatures is polymer clay, an incredibly versatile and inexpensive medium that is easy to find in craft stores. With a little imagination and ingenuity, you can sculpt polymer clay to look like just about any food you can imagine. You'll get a full primer on basic sculpting techniques, and since creating *wearable* miniature food is a unique undertaking, you'll also learn basic jewelry-making techniques to transform the miniatures into finished jewelry.

The majority of the book is comprised of "recipes" for making tiny polymer clay foods, divided into five chapters: Fresh Fruit, Morning Favorites, Savory Entrees, Sweet-Tooth Delights and Other Treats, and Holiday Goodies. The recipes progress from easy to more complex, and each chapter builds on previous concepts while gradually introducing new techniques. Each recipe lists the "ingredients" needed, with actual size illustrations of the clay so you can quickly and easily hold up a ball to the page to see how much you need. Many recipes also include suggestions for alternative flavors or colors, so you can customize the tiny foods to reflect your real favorites. We strongly encourage you to create pizza with the toppings you like and whip up your favorite flavor cupcake! In keeping with the cookbook theme, each chapter also has a real food recipe (yes, one you can actually eat) for a favorite dish we thought you might enjoy.

We hope you have a lot of fun creating and wearing these projects—and enjoying the memories they bring. *Bon appetit!*

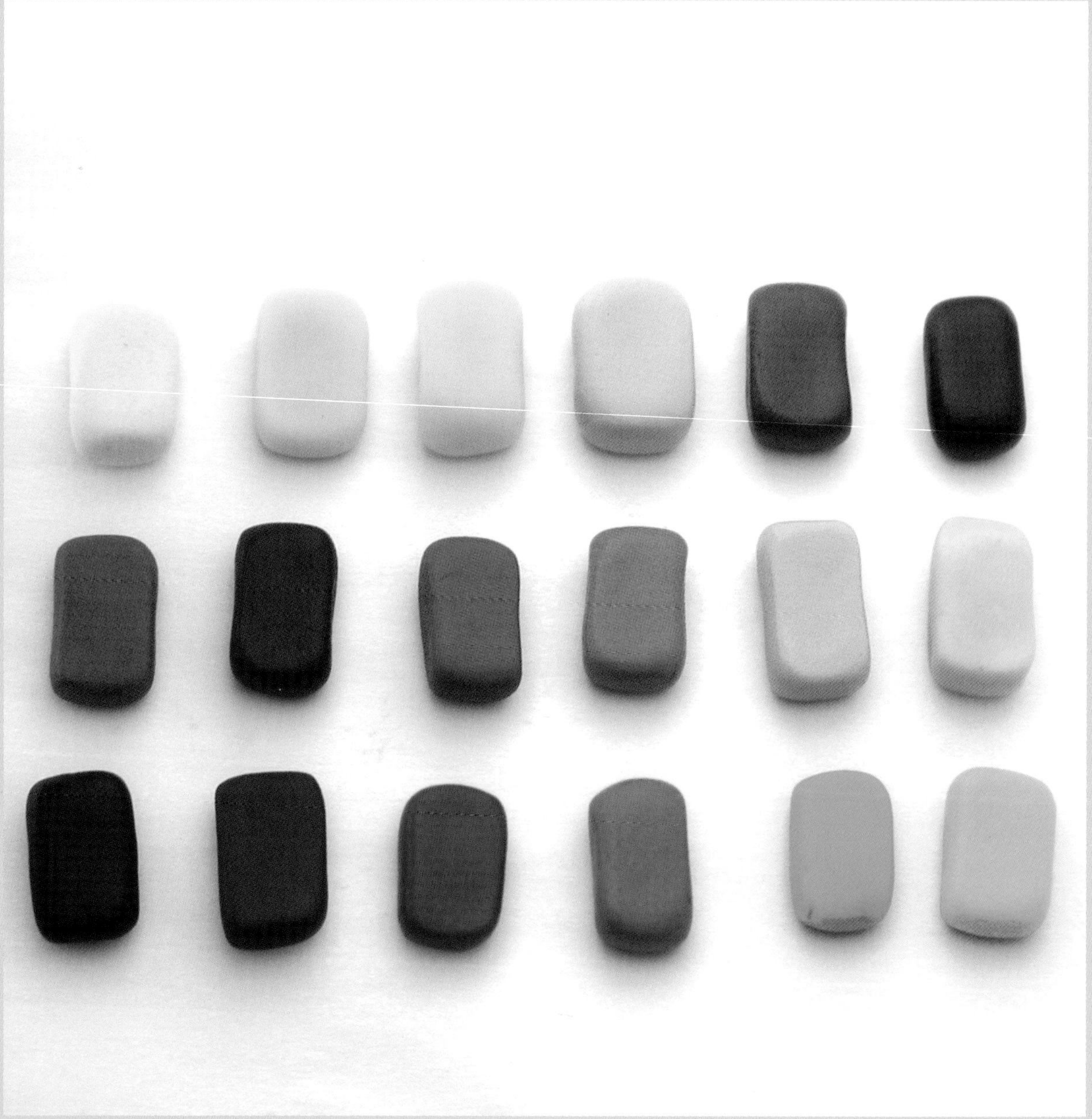

1

Clay Cookery Basics

Over time, we've picked up all kinds of tricks to working with polymer clay, and each of us has developed her own way of working. Here, we describe how we find it easiest to work, but don't take our word as dogma; there are as many ways of doing things as there are polymer clay artists. The more you practice and experiment with clay, the more you'll learn and develop your own techniques. Above all, feel free to play! One of the best things about polymer clay is that if you don't like what you've made, you can always squish it down and begin again.

Stocking the Pantry: What You'll Need

Polymer clay is a fantastic, almost endlessly variable artistic medium. The clay itself is inexpensive, and it's easy to start working with it since you'll need only a few basic tools and supplies. Most of our favorite sculpting tools are general household items. We've outlined all the tools and materials we use in this book below. We also definitely encourage you to keep an eye out for other items you can use to create interesting textures and shapes.

Polymer Clay

A great analogy for the structure of polymer clay is sand at the beach. When dry, sand is millions of individual little particles. If you add water, the consistency changes into something you can use to sculpt sand castles. If you add a lot of water, that sand takes on an almost soupy texture, and you can use it for creating drip decorations on your castle. If you had an oven big and hot enough, you could bake the castle. All the water would burn off and the grains of sand would melt together into glass. If, instead, you let your castle dry out, all that water would evaporate and the castle would crumble back into a million grains of sand.

Polymer clay works much the same way, only the tiny grains are a form of PVC (think of those white pipes you see in the plumbing section of a hardware store, or the surface of a raincoat), and the water is an oily substance called plasticizer. When you bake your polymer clay pieces, the plasticizer burns off in the oven and the individual particles of PVC fuse together to create a sturdy finished sculpture.

There are numerous brands of polymer clay, but the three most commonly available ones are Premo, Fimo, and Sculpey III. You should be able to find polymer clay and tools at nearly any local craft store. There are also a couple of good websites that have clay and tools for sale. See page 159 for some of our suggestions.

There are a lot of brands of polymer clay, but we think Premo is the best.

Premo is our favorite brand, since it has a wonderful consistency straight from the package and a predictable color mixing, and is very durable once baked. Although it is the most expensive brand you'll find at your local craft store, the difference in quality is worth the price (and it does frequently go on sale). We created all the recipes in this book using Premo, with the occasional bit of Sculpey where noted.

Sculpey III is the least expensive of the brands, and has the most premixed colors. But it tends to be very soft from the package, and can get downright mushy if you overwork it. Many of the colors are fine to use in place of Premo. There are several colors you'll want to avoid, however. The orange and white tend to burn easily. The yellow has an oddly phosphorescent effect; you're better off with Premo cadmium yellow. You also do not want to buy Sculpey (no numbers) in the one-pound box at the craft store. While the clay is the same basic medium, this is peachy-colored clay for doll-making and has a slightly different consistency and finish.

Fimo is the middle ground between Premo and Sculpey III, and comes in two different formulations: classic and soft. As the names suggest, Classic Fimo is very firm, while Fimo Soft is much more workable straight from the package. The colors for both are comparable to Premo, although they do not mix in

Clay-Be-Gone Sugar Scrub

We started making this scrub a few years ago, and now always have a jar of it around. It's great for getting clay off your hands and leaves your skin feeling soft and clean.

$1/8$ cup (30 ml) salt
$1/4$ cup (60 ml) granulated sugar
$1/4$ cup (60 ml) liquid soap
$1/8$ cup (30 ml) olive oil
Clean jelly jar

YIELD: JUST UNDER 1 CUP OF SCRUB

Add the salt and sugar to the jelly jar. Stir to mix.

Add the liquid soap and olive oil on top, then use a fork to thoroughly mix the salt/sugar mixture into the soap/olive oil. It helps to scoop upward from the bottom to the top instead of just stirring. The mixture will be thick and granular, and look pale and a bit frothy.

TO USE: Scoop a small amount of scrub (about as much as will fit on your index finger) and massage across your hands while still dry. This should remove most of the clay residue. Add a bit of water, finish washing, and rinse. Dry your hands with a lint-free cloth. We use a clean old pillowcase cut into hand-towel size pieces. Just avoid a flannel case as it will leave lots of lint on your hands.

quite the same way. Fimo also has a slightly lower baking temperature than the other two (see baking section later in the chapter on pages 24–25).

Different brands of clay can be mixed together as well. Just be sure to mix them thoroughly and bake your finished piece using whichever brand's suggested temperature is lowest.

Polymer clay is also available as a thick liquid, which is great for creating flowing effects, such as drizzly frosting. The majority of clay used in this book is the solid form, but we also use liquid clay in two ways: as a surface effect, since it wonderfully mimics the texture of sauces and frostings, and structurally, as a bonding agent or reinforcement for delicate pieces. In its uncured state, liquid clay looks slightly foggy, but it cures to a surprisingly transparent finish. The thinner the layer of liquid clay, the more transparent it will be once baked.

Work Surface

We like to use a big 8 x 8-inch (20 x 20-cm) smooth white flooring tile as our work surface. Tiles are easy to clean, inexpensive, don't react with the clay, and can be baked in the oven. You can find them at any home improvement store. We like the ones that are pure white because it is easy to see any color residue or dirt on the tile, which makes it easy to keep them clean.

We can't emphasize enough the importance of a clean work surface. Any little surface dust or lint will stick to your clay, and you'll end up with unwanted speckles in your finished pieces. Or, if you roll white clay over a tile that has a bit of red residue, you'll end up with more of a pink color—not necessarily what you want for your miniature whipped cream! Make sure you wipe down your working tile before and after you work with your clay to avoid getting lots of clay residue or little linty fibers in your work.

To clean your tile, splash a bit of rubbing alcohol onto the surface. Rubbing alcohol dissolves the clay, so it is also useful for cleaning paintbrushes used for liquid clay. Wipe your tile clean and dry with a lint-free cloth. We like to use a piece of old pillowcase (not flannel). Paper towels also work, but a dedicated clay cloth is nice since it wastes fewer paper towels!

To clean your hands, we recommend using a sugar scrub (see recipe on page 13). The sugar and salt in the scrub act like a softer version of sand or pumice to scrub off clay residue from your hands, especially when the clay is stuck down in the valleys of your fingerprint ridges. Sugar and salt are also colorless and dissolve completely in water, so your hands will be nice and clean, free of dyes and random particles when you're working with the clay. We recommend thoroughly washing your hands before you begin any project so they're free of dust and dirt. We also strongly recommend that you wash your hands after finishing a project, especially before you eat.

Sculpting Tools

You don't need fancy tools for sculpting with polymer clay; your hands will be doing most of the work! You will, however, need help from some basic household items to create certain effects and textures. Many of our favorite tools are everyday items such as pins, toothpicks, razor blades, even blunt pencils. With a little creativity you can almost always find something around the house to create the texture or shape you want! A safety pin usually works just as well as a needle tool, for example. The tool we use for a given project is often a reflection of our personal preferences. For example, Jessica prefers a needle tool while Susan prefers a straight pin. Either works equally well, so experiment to find the tool that works best for you. If you prefer the fancier version, you can find it at most craft stores or online.

There are three broad categories of tools that we use for sculpture: fine-point tools, rounded-end tools, and cutting tools.

Fine-point tools. We use three fine-point tools: a safety pin, a needle tool, and a stippling tool. The

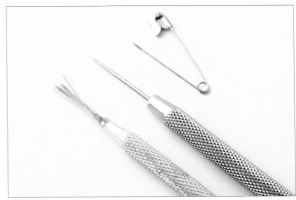

You'll need some fine-point tools to make the projects: a safety pin, needle tool, and stippling tool (from top to bottom).

fine points on the safety pin and the needle tool are completely interchangeable. We use these tools for two basic purposes: we use the tip of the tool to create tiny indentations in the surface of the clay, and we use the side to create straight lines. The stippling tool is basically just a collection of stiff, fine wires in a handle. It creates lots of tiny indentations simultaneously, so we use it as a time-saving tool for projects that require lots of tiny indentations, such as the lemon rind or cupcake.

We also use the needle tool in one other way: the grip of the tool has a nice waffle pattern that is perfect for creating the texture on the outside of an ice cream cone.

Rounded-end tools. The three rounded-point tools we use are the ball end of a straight pin, a tooth-

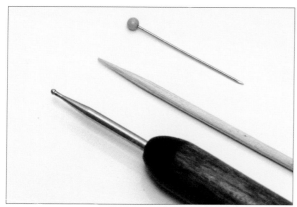

The ball end of a straight pin, a toothpick, and a double-ball stylus (from top to bottom) are the rounded-end tools you'll need.

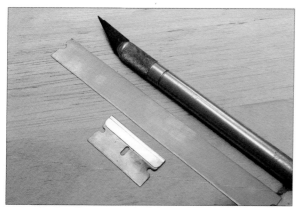

The cutting tools you'll need are a utility knife, a tissue blade, and a razor blade (from top to bottom).

pick, and a double-ball stylus. The double-ball stylus is a very handy tool that has two different-sized metal balls, one on each end of a central handle. Rounded-end tools are useful for creating large, smooth indentations in the clay, such as the top of the apple or the hole in a bagel. They are also useful for smoothly shaping the clay.

Cutting tools. The three cutting tools used in this book are a utility knife, a tissue blade, and a razor blade. These tools are all used for cleanly cutting or slicing the clay. The utility knife is useful for cutting very small pieces, such as sprinkles or pieces of salt for the pretzel. The razor blade and tissue blade are completely interchangeable. The only difference between the two is that the tissue blade has a thinner and more flexible blade, so it sometimes gives more precise cuts than a razor blade.

We also use two small round paintbrushes (size 4 is perfect): one for working with liquid clay, the other for dabbing on powdered soft pastel. To keep them separate, we use a white nylon brush for the liquid clay and a reddish taklon brush for the pastel. If you'd like to purchase only one paintbrush, keep it clean by washing it in rubbing alcohol after use.

Other Materials

There are a couple of color effects that require some different materials to be mixed into the clay or applied to the surface.

Spices. We use two kinds of real spices, ground allspice and finely ground black pepper, to create

Just a touch of powered mica will make your charms sparkle.

Soft pastels are great for creating that perfectly browned, fresh-from-the-oven look.

speckled effects in the clay. As an added bonus, while you're working with spiced clay, it smells delicious! Mixing in the spices takes a bit more conditioning than mixing two colors of clay, since the spices are somewhat reluctant to bond with clay. Keep working the mixture, however, and the spices will eventually become evenly distributed.

Powdered mica. To create a sparkly, pearlescent effect, mix in a small amount of powdered mica with your clay.

Soft pastels. To create a baked or toasted look on pieces such as the bagel, waffle, burger bun, and pizza crust, we dab on an uneven layer of powdered soft pastel. Soft pastels are the chalky ones that come in a rainbow of colors. The one you'll use most frequently is a raw sienna, which is the color that looks like a combination of red, orange, and brown.

Oil pastels. In some cases, we add color using oil pastels instead of brushing on the soft pastel powder. Depending on the piece, you may draw the color directly onto the surface of the clay, which creates a richer, deeper surface color than the pigment powder. We also use some of the other colors for tinting the clay for sauces and frostings.

Applying Powdered Soft Pastels

Rub the pastel against a clean scrap piece of paper to produce a small pile of powdered pigment.

Gently dab your brush in the pile of powdered pastel to pick up a small amount of the pigment.

Apply the pastel to the surface of your miniature to make it look perfectly browned, as if it is fresh from the oven.

Working with Clay: Basic Techniques

We'll start with a review of basic considerations of how to work with the clay for those who have never worked with polymer clay before or those who need a quick refresher. This section will cover how to get the clay into a workable sculpting condition, how to add color and a variety of color effects, and how to form the basic shapes we'll refer to throughout the book.

Conditioning the Clay

The first step in working with polymer clay is called conditioning. Conditioning is simply getting the clay to the right working temperature and consistency for sculpting. As a general rule, the warmer the clay gets, the softer it becomes. For sculpting fine detail (such as miniature foods), you want to make the clay soft enough to work with but not so mushy that it can't hold details. Ideally, the clay will be about the texture of firm chewing gum.

Everyone has his or her own style of conditioning. Basically, you want to roll the clay into a ball, flatten it, fold it back over itself, and then roll it into a ball again. Most fresh clay is nearly ready to sculpt straight from the package. Some clay takes

See how the edges are split (left)? This means your clay needs to be conditioned more. When the edges are nice and smooth, the clay is ready to be sculpted (right).

a bit longer to condition, particularly Fimo Classic or clay that has been sitting around in your craft bin for a few years. Small amounts of clay are easy to condition in your palms. If, however, you decide you'd like to work on a much larger scale (an entire package of clay at a time, for example), you might consider investing in a pasta machine to do your kneading for you.

To determine whether your clay is ready to work with, flatten the ball into a pancake. The edges of your pancake should be nice and smooth, not cracked. The center of your pancake should yield to some pressure but not completely flatten when pressed or stick to your fingertips when you pull them away. If the edges of your pancake split, continue conditioning your clay until it is a bit warmer.

If your clay is either too soft or very crumbly, see the troubleshooting section on page 27 for suggestions on how to remedy the problem.

Working with Color

Polymer clay, like paint, comes in a full spectrum of colors. The colors we use most frequently are shown here. All are Premo except two (ivory and Granny Smith), which are Sculpey. The top row represents the neutral colors (left to right): white, ivory, translucent, ecru, raw sienna, and burnt umber. These neutral colors are the ones we use most frequently; one or more are used in nearly every project. We use the neutral colors in their straight-from-the-package state, and as bases for many other colors.

Here are all the polymer clay colors used for the projects.

The second row is the warm colors (left to right): magenta, alizarin crimson, cadmium red, orange, cadmium yellow, and zinc yellow. The alizarin crimson and cadmium red are particularly intense and tend to stain your hands, so be vigilant about washing your hands between colors when you're working with either of them.

The third row is the cool colors (left to right): black, purple, ultramarine, cobalt blue, green, and Granny Smith. We use the blues the least frequently of all of the colors since there is a surprising lack of blue foods (blueberry muffins notwithstanding!). You can create a close approximation of the Granny Smith by mixing zinc yellow and green, if you prefer to make your own. The green and purple clays are much easier to purchase premixed to ensure the highest saturated color.

There are also two kinds of special-effect clays. Pearl and metallic clays have powdered mica mixed in, which makes them a bit sparkly. In terms of color-mixing, pearl behaves almost identically to white, except that it gives a hint of subtle sparkle to the finished mixture.

Glow-in-the-dark clay looks similar to translucent clay in its unbaked form. Once baked, the unmixed clay remains a cool off-white shade but will glow green if exposed to bright light and then placed in the dark. You can mix a tiny amount of another color with glow-in-the-dark clay and it will retain its glow effect. If you add too much of another color, the phosphorescence will become diluted and the clay will lose its ability to glow.

Color Mixing

We mix colors in two primary ways: thoroughly and marbled. Thorough color mixing is exactly what it sounds like: kneading the clays together to create a uniform color without any residual streaks, such as mixing a small ball of cadmium red with a larger ball of cadmium yellow to create a uniform orange.

In real life, many foods, such as lettuce or caramel swirl ice cream, are not a uniform color. For these projects we'll marble the clay. Marbling simply means deliberately incomplete color mixing that preserves lots of streaks.

The yellow and the red balls of clay have been mixed thoroughly to create a uniform ball of orange.

Marbling Two Colors Together

Roll the two balls of clay into snakes of equal length.

Twist the two snakes together.

Wad the twisted snake into a ball. Roll the ball until it is smooth.

Roll the ball out into a snake again, twisting as you go. This process will create a wonderfully streaky piece of clay.

Lightening and Darkening

Traditionally, to lighten (tint) or darken (shade) a hue, white, translucent, clear or black is added to a fully saturated color to reduce its intensity. Adding white turns the clay a more pastel color. Adding translucent clay dilutes the color intensity. And adding dark clay makes the color look increasingly dark and sooty. The images here show what we mean.

Since the projects in this book focus on food, you'll find that we get more natural tints and shades by mixing pure saturated colors with neutral tones or a little bit of brown.

The more white you add to red clay, the more pastel pink it becomes.

As you add more translucent clay to red clay, the intensity of the red becomes more and more diluted.

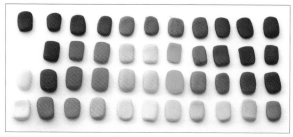

This compares the effects of adding black, white, and translucent to colored clay. Row two shows the fully saturated colors. Row one has a tiny amount of black mixed in. Row three is mixed with translucent, and row four is mixed with white.

Creating New Colors

Polymer clay mixes much the same way as oil paint. A detailed discussion of color theory is beyond the scope of this book, but you can easily find color-mixing guidelines for pigments at your local library or online. Or, even better, experiment! You'll find you can get every imaginable hue from the grocery store, and beyond.

Adding Color to Liquid Clay

Liquid clay is translucent straight from the bottle. Some projects call for colored liquid clay, such as the frosting for a cinnamon roll. The fastest way to tint liquid clay is to mix in small flakes of colored oil pastel. Oil pastels come in every imaginable color, and a little bit of oil pastel goes a long way in tinting the liquid clay.

Coloring Liquid Clay

Here's how to create a colored liquid clay mixture:

Shave a few flakes of the oil pastel onto your tile.

Add several drops of liquid clay, then stir the pastel and clay together with a clean tooth-pick. Break up the clumps of pastel until you have a uniform-colored liquid clay.

Sculpting Techniques

Now that you've assembled your tools and ingredients, let's get on to the fun part and start working with the clay! This section will cover how to create basic shapes and textures, as well as baking, quenching, and finishing the clay.

Making Shapes

There are five basic shapes we use throughout the book: a sphere, a pancake, a cylinder, a sheet, and a snake or log.

Spheres are made by gently rolling the clay between the palms of your hands. By applying even pressure and keeping your hands an even distance apart, you can roll clay into a smooth sphere without any creases or fingerprints. Every project begins with small spheres of clay, so this is an important skill to learn.

Pancakes are formed by first rolling the clay into a sphere and then pressing the sphere flat between your fingertips or against your tile. If you are creating a very thin disk, flatten the sphere into a disk in your hands instead of on your tile since the clay will become distorted when you try to peel it off your work surface.

Cylinders begin as spheres. Roll the sphere against your tile, then set it up on one end. Press

Sphere   Pancake   Cylinder

Sheet

Snake

down gently to create a crisp cylinder shape. You can keep lightly rolling and pressing down on the cylinder until you are happy with the shape.

Sheets are flattened, rectangular pieces of clay. The easiest way to create a sheet is to flatten a sphere into a thick pancake, then pinch the edges of the pancake into a square. Continue flattening and squaring off the pancake in your hands until you have a uniformly thin sheet of clay.

Snakes or *logs* are basically long strings of clay that can be used in a variety of ways. For the projects in this book, you'll need to create both thick and very thin snakes, all of which require the same process. To create a snake, begin to roll out a sphere as if you were making a cylinder, but keep rolling until you reach the desired length or width of the snake. Roll over all parts of the clay to get an even width throughout.

Adding Texture

Real food often has interesting textures. Think about a lemon peel or a cupcake. The lemon peel isn't entirely smooth; it has lots of tiny pores. Once you've gotten the shape of your piece right you can use your tools to create these textures. We also encourage you to experiment!

Sculpting for Jewelry-making

The main difference between making miniatures for your dollhouse and ones to turn into jewelry is that dollhouse miniatures can be much more delicate. Jewelry miniatures need to be a bit sturdier to stand up to multiple wearings. To prevent delicate parts such as stems and leaves from chipping off, make sure all the leaves and other thin, delicate elements are either flush with a larger surface (such as a leaf pressed onto the surface of an apple) or reinforced with wire (such as the stick on the lollipop or the stem of the apple). To make miniatures into charms, we'll also sculpt headpins, or loops of metal into the clay, so they can be turned into jewelry.

Baking

Baking polymer clay is easy. All the projects in this book require less than 20 minutes of baking time. While we give specific times and temperatures, please note that our times are consistent for baking with Premo; other brands may vary slightly, so be sure to read the directions on the package. You'll need three things to bake your pieces: an oven, an oven thermometer, and a tile covered with parchment paper.

You can bake your pieces in a conventional oven or small toaster oven that you set aside specifically for that purpose. Definitely do not bake your pieces in a microwave oven! Before baking any charms, test your oven's temperature with an oven thermometer, since all ovens tend to run a little hot or cool. If you find an inconsistency in your oven, it's better to bake your piece at a lower temperature for a little longer (such as 265° F [130° C] for 20 minutes instead of 275° F [135° C] for 15 minutes) to avoid scorching.

We also recommend keeping a close eye on your piece the first few times you bake to ensure you don't accidentally burn your hard work!

We recommend baking your pieces on a tile covered with parchment paper. The tile acts just like a pizza stone: it holds heat and evenly distributes it, which helps keep the temperature around your pieces consistent. Toaster ovens in particular can have dramatic temperature fluctuations, and the tile will greatly help even them out. Parchment paper acts as a nonstick surface between your piece and the tile. You can bake on your sculpting tile directly (without parchment paper), but you will find that your piece will have a small shiny spot where it rested against the tile. Since tiles are so inexpensive, it's easiest to just have two: one for sculpting and one that you cover with parchment paper for baking. Lastly, make sure you bake your piece in a well-ventilated area.

Quenching

This is a cool technique that makes your finished pieces extra-strong. While your pieces are baking, get a clean metal soup can from the recycling bin and fill the bottom with ice and cold water. (Please use metal, as glass and certain plastics can shatter with changes in temperature.) When your pieces come out of the oven, carefully drop them straight into the ice-cold water and let them soak for a couple of minutes. Take the cooled pieces out of the water and dry them on a towel before glazing. Your pieces will be extra-hardened by this process, and even sturdier to wear.

Glazing

Your finished piece does not necessarily need glaze. However, a simple glaze will often bring out the full depth of color, as well as add an extra layer of shine.

Sculpey makes a small jar of glaze, which is usually found adjacent to the blocks of polymer clay in craft stores. Sculpey glaze is formulated to work specifically with polymer clay. Many other types of glaze, as well as clear nail polish, can react badly with the clay and may actually start to dissolve it over time.

To glaze your piece, make sure it is cool and dry (after quenching!). Carefully paint an even layer of glaze onto your piece. Try not to put too much glaze on it or you'll get drips and an uneven coat. One trick is to grip the headpin with a large binder clip so you can cover all sides of a piece with glaze at once. The binder clip can be used to keep the charm suspended until the glaze is dry, which usually takes about a half hour.

This image shows unglazed pie on the left and glazed pie on the right.

Storing Clay

Your clay will stay clean and useable for a very long

time if you store it properly. We have clay in our stash that is well over fifteen years old and still useable. The best way to store blocks of clay is in resealable airtight bags. Don't mix colors in the same bag, as you'll find they'll stick together very quickly. Also, squeeze as much air as possible out of the bags before you close them. We find it helpful to keep the original packaging with the colors, in case we want to remember the brand, baking information, or specific color name.

If you're like us, you'll soon start to collect a whole rainbow of small portions of mixed colors and half-completed projects. We have tiles covered in little blobs of scrap clay. We keep the scrap tiles in small airtight plastic containers to prevent the pieces from drying out and to keep pesky dust off the clay. Tupperware from garage sales is great for this purpose!

Troubleshooting

We know most of you will dive right into the projects without reading this section. That's great, and we encourage it! However, sooner or later you will probably run into one of the following problems. When you do, this section is here to help you out!

The clay is too soft. The most common reason for clay being too soft is that it has been overworked or over-conditioned. The more you work the clay in your hands, the warmer it will become. Eventually, it will get sticky and react to the smallest amount of pressure, which makes it impossible to sculpt. The easiest solution is simply to set your clay aside for half an hour so it has a chance to cool. If you have especially warm hands, or find that many of your projects become mushy, consider allowing a cool-down break between steps.

If your clay is sticky and mushy right out of the package, there may be too much plasticizer in the clay. To stiffen the clay, flatten it into a thick pancake and sandwich it between two sheets of clean (unprinted) paper. Add a heavy book or another weight on top and let it sit for a few hours. The pressure from the weight will help the paper leach some of the plasticizer from the clay. The paper will have an oily stain, and your clay should be stiffer when you knead it.

The clay is crumbly. If your clay crumbles in your hands while you're trying to knead it, one of two things may have happened: either your clay dried out, or it became partially heat cured.

First, your clay may have simply dried out a bit. The plasticizer very, very gradually evaporates if the clay is left out and exposed to air. To prevent clay from drying out, keep it tightly wrapped in plastic

Note the oily stain this clay has left, which shows that it had too much plasticizer in it.

Don't toss your crumbly clay. It can sometimes be restored to softness.

wrap or individual plastic bags. To revive dried clay, add a few drops of clay softener. Only add a small amount at a time! Let it sit for several hours to allow the plasticizer to soak into the clay. Try kneading the clay again; it should be softer, and the crumbles should stick together again.

If adding clay softener does not help, it is possible that your clay might have already gotten partially baked. Partial baking can happen if, for example, the clay is accidentally left in the back of a car or a delivery truck on a very hot day. One major caveat to buying clay online: do not purchase clay online in the summer. There is a fairly high chance that your clay will cook in the back of the shipping trucks while en route! If you've partially baked your clay, unfortunately it can't be restored to the same condition as raw clay.

If it is chocolate brown, you can always chop it up and use it as chocolate chips. Ecru can be chopped up to use as nuts. If it is another color, you can chop it very fine, and mix it in with some other clay to use as a base for pieces that will be covered.

There are little flecks of dirt or lint fibers in the clay. Lint and dirt in the clay is incredibly frustrating! To prevent this, make sure your hands and working surface are very clean before you begin. Keep blocks of clay stored in small airtight plastic bags to prevent dust. If you are midway through a project and need to set it aside for more than a few hours, lay a clean piece of plastic wrap over your work. Lint is usually transferred from your hands to your clay directly. The fastest way to get lint on your clay is to rub your hands against your jeans or a fuzzy dark towel, then immediately work with the clay. When you wash your hands, dry them against a clean old piece of sheeting or a dishcloth you've set aside for this purpose.

If you notice lint when you begin conditioning the clay, it is probably surface lint. You can easily scrape it off. The clay underneath should be clean. Add the linty clay to your scrap pile.

If you notice the lint after sculpting your piece, but before baking it, you can try gently scraping off the flecks. Or moisten a cotton swab in rubbing alcohol and very gently swab the lint off the surface. Alcohol will dissolve the clay, so be sure to use a damp cotton swab (not a wet one), and only dab one color at a time.

If you notice the lint after you've baked your piece, try gently sanding the surface with ultra-fine grit sandpaper (such as the kind from an auto parts store). Alternatively, very gently scrape the surface with small woodcarving tools or a razor blade.

The clay has unwanted color residue. There are two common causes for color residue transfer: unwashed tiles and unwashed hands. To keep your colors distinct and clean, wash your hands and tile whenever you change from a dark color to a lighter color (particularly if you're using red) or if you've used pastels. Wash your hands thoroughly; color tends to get stuck in the valleys between finger-print ridges.

If your clay only has a small amount of color residue, you can try thoroughly mixing it. Often a tiny amount of surface color will blend into a larger ball of color undetectably. If the residue is still obvious after mixing, set aside the clay in your scrap pile. You'll eventually find a use for it!

The surface of the piece is burned. The most common cause of scorched or burned clay is an improperly calibrated oven. We strongly recommend using an oven thermometer to accurately gauge the real temperature of your oven, and watching your pieces carefully while they're baking, particularly the first few times.

If your piece is only a tiny bit scorched, try lightly sanding the surface with an ultra-fine grit sandpaper, or scraping it clean with a razor blade. Alternatively, you can try to paint your piece with acrylics to cover the darker burned spots.

If your piece is very blackened and burned, unfortunately there isn't anything you can do. It's incredibly disappointing when your hard work ends up burned to a crisp, but perhaps you can take some comfort in knowing it eventually happens to everyone!

2

Jewelry-Making 101: Tools And Techniques

Miniatures are fun on their own, but they're even more fun to wear as unique accessories. In each of the projects in this book, we show you how to make the miniature into a charm that you can turn into finished jewelry. This chapter covers the three major jewelry-making techniques you'll need to convert your miniatures into earrings, necklaces or bracelets, as well as stud earrings and rings. We've divided this chapter into three sections: wire wrapping, bead stringing, and making glued pieces.

Getting Stocked: Basic Jewelry-making Supplies

When you walk into a bead shop or the jewelry section of a craft store, it's easy to get overwhelmed by the sheer variety of beads, specialized tools, and other supplies. Fortunately, the finished projects in this book require only a few key tools and supplies to create. In fact, you don't even need many commercially-made beads since you'll be making your own! We've divided this section into the supplies you'll need for each specific kind of project—earrings, necklaces and bracelets, and glued pieces such as stud earrings and rings—so that it will be easy for you to stock up on just the supplies you'll actually need. We've included a quick list up front. For detailed descriptions of the tools and materials, please visit the relevant sections in this chapter.

Wire wrapping (charms & earrings)

- needle-nose pliers
- nail clippers
- headpins
- 24-or 26-gauge wire
- ear wires

Bead stringing (necklaces & bracelets)

- seed beads (size 11)
- clasp & catch (such as a jump ring)
- (stringing on braided wire)
    - Beadalon
    - crimp beads
    - crimping pliers

- (stringing on nylon thread)
    - nylon beading thread
    - beading needle
    - bead tips
    - bead-stringing glue

Glued pieces (stud earrings, rings)

- earring posts & nuts
- ring backing
- cyanoacrylate (super) glue
- sandpaper (220 grit)
- rubbing alcohol

Wire Wrapping: Making Charms and Earrings

Wire wrapping is used in all the jewelry projects in this book, with the exception of the stud earrings and the ring. It is the technique of making simple, securely closed loops from pieces of wire. We use wire wrapping to create the loop at the top of each miniature that turns it into a charm. The same technique is also used to fashion earrings, and to attach charms onto necklaces and bracelets.

Tools and Materials

Needle-nose pliers are used in almost every project. We recommend needle-nose pliers specifically made for jewelry-making, since they have a finer tip than those found at the hardware store. You can find them at craft stores, bead stores, or online. Pliers range in quality (and price) based on the grip/handle and tension. The most expensive pliers are more ergonomic and comfortable if you're doing a great deal of wire wrapping, but simpler pliers work just as well. We recommend that you buy a pair in the $8 to $10 range, since they will be much more comfortable and longer lasting than the very cheapest ones.

Needle-nose pliers (left) and nail clippers (right).

Nail clippers—just the plain, ordinary kind—are perfect wire cutters for the fine-gauge wire we use in this book. You can find specialized wire-cutting pliers, but we find that nail clippers work just as well and are very easy to maneuver into small spaces.

Wire comes in a variety of thicknesses, called gauges. The higher the number of the gauge, the thinner the wire. For wire wrapping, we use 26-gauge, since it is both sturdy and pliable. For beginners, silver-plated copper wire is a good choice; it is both inexpensive and easy to use. If you'd like to use sterling silver, it comes in three hardnesses: dead soft, half-hard, and hard. We prefer half-hard. If you work with sterling silver, be sure to save all of your scraps, since many jewelry supply companies will purchase scrap.

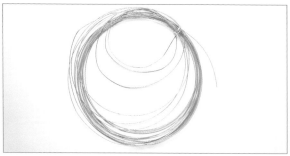

For wire wrapping, we suggest 26-gauge wire.

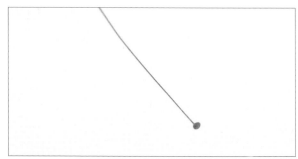

Each project specifies exactly when and where to add the headpin.

Headpins are lengths of wire with a small head on one end, like a miniature elongated nail. The head part keeps a bead from sliding off the end of the headpin. We use headpins for the same purpose, but in our case we sculpt the headpin into the charms as we make them instead of add them after the fact.

Push the headpin up into the miniature until the head part of the headpin is flush with the bottom of your piece. If you want, smooth over the bottom end with additional clay to hide the end of the headpin. Once the headpin is inserted, take care not to rotate it excessively, as this will cause the hole around your headpin to enlarge. Leave the headpin in place while you bake your piece.

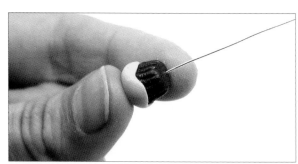

To insert a headpin, you'll usually insert the pin side through the center of the bottom of the miniature. Hold your thumb on the top of the miniature for stability, so that you can feel when the pin is about to poke through the top of the piece.

Making a Wrapped Loop

A wrapped loop is the fundamental wire wrapping structure you'll need to know how to create. Basically, it is a simple loop secured by wrapping the wire around itself. Creating consistent, clean loops takes a bit of practice, but you'll soon be a pro!

1. Start with a baked charm on a headpin. Grip the wire about $1/8$" (3.18 mm) above the top of the charm with the end of your needle-nose pliers.

2. Use your fingers to grip the very end of your wire, then wrap it around the tip of your pliers and create a loop. The tail should stick out at a 90 degree angle.

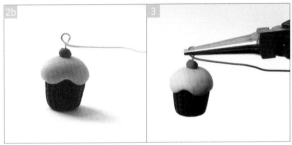

3. Remove the pliers and grip the side of the loop.

4. Hold the tail of the wire and wrap it around the exposed wire between the loop and the top of the charm. You'll want to spiral the wire downward from the loop to the top of the charm and keep the wire as tight as possible for a clean wrap. You should be able to wrap it around two to three times, depending on how much room you left in step 1.

5. Use your nail clippers to trim off the extra wire as close to your wrapped loop as possible, so there is no little piece of tail to snag anything while you're wearing your charm.

Making a Double-sided Loop

A double-sided loop is a simple variation on the wrapped loop. In this case, you're creating a piece of wire with a loop on two sides, instead of just one. We use double-sided loops when we want to attach an accent bead to a charm to give it extra sparkle.

1. Start with a straight 3" (7.6 cm) length of 26-gauge wire. Grip the wire with your needle-nose pliers so you have a 1" (2.5 cm) length on one side and a 2" (5 cm) length on the other.

2. Grip the short end of the wire with your fingers and wrap it around the end of your pliers to create a loop. The short tail should stick out at a 90 degree angle from the rest of the wire.

3. Turn the loop you've just made upside down, and slide a charm into the loop (note that the charm in this example already has a finished loop). Basically, you're creating a one-link chain, with a finished loop on the charm, and an unfinished loop on your piece of wire.

4. Grip the unfinished loop with the side of your pliers. Wrap the loop closed and trim the tail, as in steps 4 and 5 of the wrapped loop.

5. Slide an accent bead onto your wire.

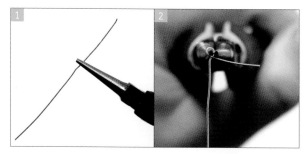

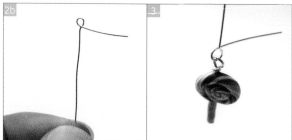

6. Create a second loop above the accent bead, wrap the loop closed, and trim the tail. You now have a charm that can be turned into earrings or added to a necklace or bracelet.

Making a Figure-Eight Loop

A figure-eight loop is a variation on the double-sided loop, used in place of a headpin when one can't be used, such as in triangular pieces of pie.

Basically, the bottom loop is sculpted into the charm and serves the same function as the head of a headpin: it is held in place by the clay that surrounds it, which prevents it from being pulled out of the finished piece. Imagine, for example, taking a lollipop and inserting the stick end into a clay piece. If you pulled on the lollipop at the top, the stick would pull out of the clay. But if you inserted the lollipop end into the clay and then baked the piece, it would hold securely when pulled.

1. Take a 24-gauge piece of wire that is about 1½" (3.8 cm) long (this is a great way to use the discarded tails from headpins).

2. Make a loop at one end.

3. Make a loop at the other end and wrap the second loop closed.

4. Trim off the short tail.

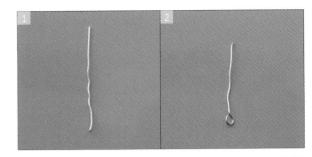

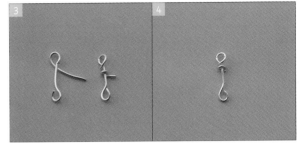

In your finished piece, you'll want the insertion point for the figure-eight loop to be hidden as much as possible. Before baking, insert the bottom loop into your piece vertically and then twist the loop 90 degrees so it is horizontal. Gently press down on the charm to close up the cut made by the loop.

This will allow the clay inside your charm to get a better grip on the loop, making it sturdier. The best time to insert a figure-eight piece into a charm will vary according to the project, so each project that uses one will have specific instructions.

Adding Ear Wires

Ear wires are the pieces that go through your earlobes to create dangly earrings. They come in a variety of metals. Surgical steel wire is hypoallergenic and the least expensive. It can be tough to work with for wire wrapping, though, since it is the stiffest of the metals commonly used in jewelry-making.

Sterling silver wire is made of at least 92.5 percent pure silver. The other 7.5 percent is usually copper. Pure silver is a very soft metal, so copper is usually mixed in to make it a bit stiffer and less likely to scratch. Many sterling silver findings will be stamped somewhere with a tiny "925," indicating that they are truly sterling silver.

Silver-plated wires are a base metal with a very thin coating of sterling silver. Base metal simply means that the metal is not a precious one (such as silver, platinum, or gold). Silver-plated pieces are much less expensive than sterling silver. The down side is that the layer of silver is very thin, so it will rub off over time, showing the metal underneath. We don't recommend silver-plated ear wires, since most

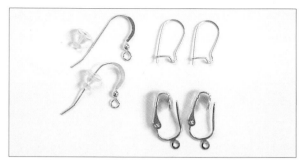

Three different types of ear wires: French hooks (left), kidney wires (top right), and clip-ons (bottom right).

manufacturers don't specify what the base metal is, and often that base metal contains nickel or other metals to which many people are allergic. If sterling silver ear wires are too expensive, you're better off getting surgical steel wires instead.

There are three main styles of ear wires: French hook, kidney, and clip-on. Stud earrings are structurally quite different, so we cover how to create them in a separate section on page 46.

French hooks are a more traditional style, shaped like fishhooks that are open in the back. They should be worn with rubber backings to keep them securely in your ears. Kidney wires can be hooked closed to keep the earrings secure without any rubber backings. Clip-on earrings are great for those without pierced ears.

Finishing dangly earrings takes two quick steps once your charms are finished: wrapping an accent bead into a double-sided loop above each charm, then securing the wrapped accent pieces onto ear wires. To wrap the accent bead onto double-sided loops, see page 36.

To finish earrings on kidney wires, simply slide the top loop of your accented charm onto the wire, and let it fall into the little notch at the front.

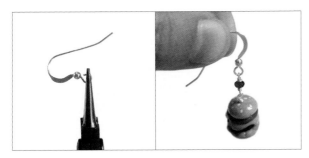

To add your earring to a French hook or clip-on ear wire, open the loop on the bottom of the wire by twisting it to the side. Then slide your accented charm into the open loop, and twist the loop closed again.

Bead Stringing: Making Necklaces and Bracelets

Colorful beads complement these charms really well, and it's easy to make simple beaded bracelets and necklaces. There are two main materials that you can string beads on: braided steel and nylon. We'll cover the techniques for working with each in turn after we cover the basics of beading in general.

Tools and Materials

Beads. There are an enormous variety of bead sizes, materials, and colors available today. For the projects in this book we use two kinds of beads: seed beads and accent crystals. Seed beads are

From top to bottom: size 15 seed beads, size 11 seed beads, size 8 seed beads, and 4mm Swarovski crystal bicones.

tiny beads usually made from glass. They are sized based on approximately how many are needed to cover 1 inch of stringing material, so the higher the number, the smaller the bead. The smallest size we use is 15, since we find beads smaller than that difficult to string. We usually use size 11 for necklaces and bracelets, and size 8 as accents. Swarovski or Czech crystals come in a variety of sizes as well, but we usually use 3mm or 4mm bicones to add just a touch of sparkle to our designs.

Clasps are necessary to open and close your necklace or bracelet, unless you're making a very long necklace or don't plan to remove your bracelet. There are several types of clasps available, with closures that twist, clip, and snap together. The two types we use in this book are lobster clasps and spring rings. We prefer to use lobster clasps, since their elongated shape and hinge tend to open with more ease. Lobster clasps have a single closed loop

Lobster claw clasp (top), spring ring clasp (bottom), closed jump ring (right).

that is the attachment point for your strung piece. Regardless of the style of clasp you use, you'll also need a corresponding loop for the clasp to latch on to; generally this is a closed jump ring.

Jump rings are small metal loops that can be used either as the catch for clasps or as connectors between a charm and a necklace or bracelet. There are two types of jump rings: open and closed. The difference between open and closed jump rings is that open jump rings can be twisted open while closed jump rings are permanently soldered shut. Closed jump rings are more secure to use as a catch for clasps, since they cannot be pulled open with tension.

Use your pliers to gently twist open the ring on the spring ring to attach a charm.

Spring rings are handy little hybrids of traditional clasps and jump rings. They feature a clasp element for the main top loop, but have a second small loop that can be twisted open to attach a charm. Spring rings are traditionally used as clasps, but they're also a great substitute for jump rings since you can easily slide the spring ring onto a necklace chain to create a simple necklace without any tools.

Stringing on Braided Steel Wire

Braided steel wire. Stringing on braided wire is a very secure way to bead, since the braided steel takes quite a bit of force to break. We particularly recommend using wire if you're creating pieces for kids. Bead-stringing wire comes in a variety of thicknesses, finishes, and drapes. The higher the number of strands in the wire, the more gently the wire drapes. We usually use a bright finish, 7-strand wire.

Crimping pliers are the most specialized tool you'll need. If you plan to string beads onto braided steel wire, you'll need these pliers to finish the ends. There is really no substitute for these pliers since they are specifically designed for the purpose. You can find them at most craft stores in the jewelry section.

Crimps are small metal seed beads with an extra-

We like Beadalon stringing wire, but there are other brands as well. Crimping pliers are the perfect tool to help you secure the ends of your beading wire.

large hole in the middle. When properly folded around the ends of stringing wire with your crimping pliers, crimp beads function the same way a knot does: the beads prevent the wire from coming loose from the clasp.

Stringing on Nylon

Nylon thread. Stringing on nylon thread is a great option when you want your finished pieces to have a nice drape. Braided nylon is a very sturdy, non-stretchy type of thread. You can find it sold under various names, such as Silamide or Dandyline.

Bead tips are nifty findings to use when you're stringing on nylon thread: they hide the final knots on either end of your strung piece and serve as the attachment point between your piece and a clasp.

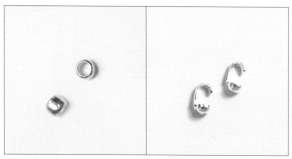
Crimping beads (left) and bead tips (right).

Beading needles. These are very fine, thin needles that can both hold your thread and slide easily through the tiny holes in seed beads. We particularly like extra-large eye beading needles, since they are very easy to thread.

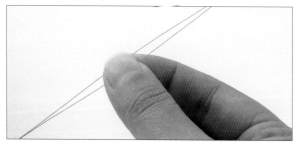
Beading needles make it easy to quickly string beads on nylon thread.

Bead-stringing glue. This is a secure yet flexible glue that seals the knots in your bead tips to make them durable.

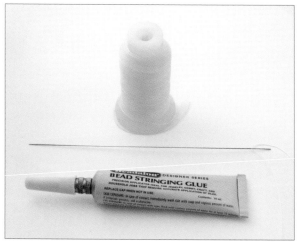
Bead-stringing glue keeps your knots secure and safe from fraying.

Figuring Out the Right Length for Bracelets and Necklaces

To determine the correct length for a bracelet, wrap a measuring tape around your wrist, over the wrist bone. Add about ½ inch (1.25 cm)to this measurement—that will be approximately the right length for your bracelet. Your bracelet should be loose enough to put on, but not so loose that it can slide off.

If you're making a bracelet for someone else, a 7½- to 8-inch (19- to 20-cm) bracelet will be about the right size for most adult women. Kids aged 5 to 8 usually wear a 6- to 6½-inch (15- to 16.5-cm) bracelet, and larger kids and smaller adult wrists will fall around the base of the collarbone on most adult women. For kids, a 15-inch (38-cm) necklace is normally a good length; it's not too long, but they can also grow into it.

How to String onto Braided Steel Wire: Crimping

When stringing onto braided steel wire, you'll need to use a technique called crimping to securely fasten the ends of the wire to the clasp. To finish a piece on braided wire with crimps, you'll need: a clasp, a jump ring, crimping pliers, and crimp beads. When properly folded around the ends of the stringing wire with your crimping pliers, crimp beads function the same way a knot does to prevent the wire from coming loose from the clasp.

are 6½ to 7 inches (16.5 to 18 cm). If you're not sure of the sizing, make a small extender chain by wrapping together two double-sided loops (see page 36). Attach one end of the chain to the jump ring on your bracelet and the second end to a second jump ring. The wearer can then choose which jump ring to attach the clasp to for a great fit.

To determine the correct length for a necklace, loop a piece of string or measuring tape around your neck. If you're making a necklace for someone else, a 16- to 18-inch (41- to 46-cm) necklace

1. Start by cutting a length of wire about 3 " (7.6 cm) longer than the length of the piece you're making. This will leave you extra wire to work with.

2. Slip one end of the wire through the closed loop on your clasp, then through a crimp bead.

3. Leaving a 1" (2.5 cm) tail of wire, slide the crimp bead up until it is about ⅛" (3.2 cm) from your clasp.

4. To secure the crimp bead, you'll need crimping pliers. Crimping pliers have three important working spaces: a U-shaped notch at the back, an oval notch

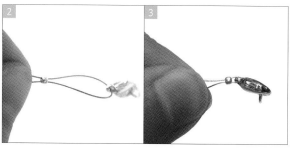

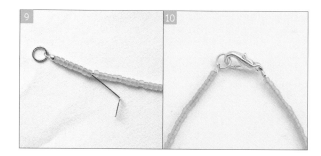

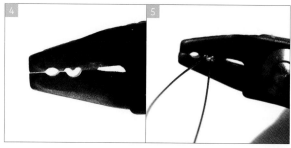

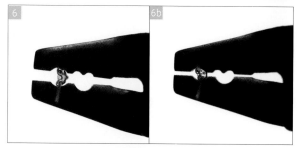

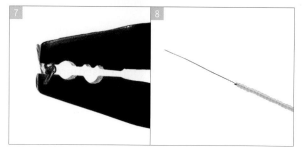

in the middle, and a flat space at the very tip.

5. Keeping the two wires separate and parallel, squish the crimp bead in the U-shaped notch first. Your two wires should be separated by a little valley of metal.

6. Turn your "U" 90 degrees, and insert it into the oval notch on the pliers. Squish down to stack the two wires on top of each other. Your crimp will now be slightly rounded.

7. Move your crimp to the very front of the pliers and squeeze it between the flat space to flatten the crimp bead and create a very secure hold.

8. String your beads over the two pieces of wire to secure the tail. Continue beading until you reach your desired length. Slide on a crimp bead at the end.

9. Wrap the tail of your wire through the jump ring, then back through the crimp bead and about ½" (13 mm) of seed beads.

10. Crimp the second crimp bead just as you did the first. Trim any remaining wire tail.

How to String onto Nylon

Stringing onto nylon is a great option when you prefer your pieces to have a nice drape while you're wearing them. Although braided wire is a bit sturdier than nylon, finishing a necklace with bead tips can offer a bit more of a polished look than a piece finished with crimps, as the bead tips conceal the ends of the string nicely in connecting with the clasps. In addition to seed beads, a clasp, and a jump ring, you'll need: nylon thread, a beading needle, bead-stringing glue, and two bead tips.

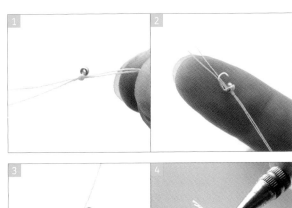

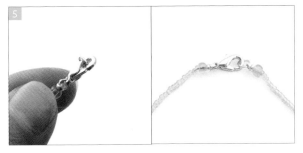

1. Thread your beading needle with a double length of thread about 4" (102 mm) longer than your desired finished length. Knot the end of your thread and string a very small silver seed bead over the knot. Knot around this seed bead. This will create a larger knot that is more secure within your bead tip.

2. Slide a bead tip onto your thread until your knot is resting inside the cup.

3. String beads on your thread until you reach your desired length. Add a second bead tip, then knot the end of your thread the same way you did in step 1.

4. Add a few drops of bead-stringing glue to the knots in each bead tip. Wait 30 minutes to an hour for the glue to set, and then trim the loose threads from each end of your piece.

5. Slide the loop part of one bead tip through the loop on the back of your clasp. Using needle-nose pliers, curve the bead tip loop closed around the clasp loop. On the other end, close the bead tip around a jump ring or another loop in the same way.

Stringing Beads

Here is a very handy technique for stringing seed beads quickly.

1. Pour a single layer of seed beads into a muffin cup or another flat-bottomed dish.

2. Give the cup a quick shake, so all of the beads lay with their holes facing up. Press your forefinger into the beads to pick them up.

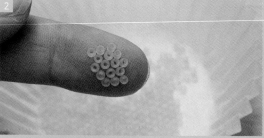

3. Hold the beads with your thumb and roll your thumb just a little against your forefinger to reorient the beads with the holes facing downward. Since all the beads will be facing the same way on your forefinger, it will be much quicker to string them.

4. Slide the beads onto your stringing material, and continue adding beads until you reach the desired length for your piece. Finish the ends as appropriate to your stringing material (see sections on pages 43–46).

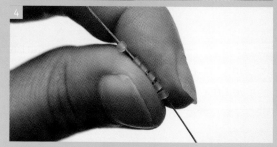

Making Stud Earrings, Rings, and Other Glued Pieces

Pieces that require a glued element, such as stud earrings or rings, are constructed in a very different way from the pieces that use headpins. You'll need to plan for the glued finding while you're still sculpting to properly prepare the area to be glued. Glued pieces should be sculpted with a shallow indentation in the back to provide a bit of mechanical hold to the metal in addition to the glue hold. Pieces made this way will be sturdier than if you glue the metal to a flat surface, since the clay will help hold the metal finding in place from the side. You need a clean, uneven surface on both attachment points.

Tools and Materials

Earring post backings are used to make stud earrings. We like ones that have 1/16-inch (4-mm) flat pads. Don't forget to get earring backs as well!

Ring. If you're making a ring, you'll need a ring base. The bases come in a variety of metals and styles.

Earring posts and ring base.

Jewelry glue. We recommend cyanoacrylate (super) glue for securing sculpted pieces to earring posts and ring backs.

Sandpaper (220 grit). Fine-grit sandpaper is useful for roughing up the smooth finish on the pad of stud earring posts and the front of ring bases.

Cotton swabs and rubbing alcohol. To get a nice, secure bond between your miniature and the metal, you'll want to make sure the surfaces to be bonded are very clean. We recommend using a cotton swab dipped in rubbing alcohol to wipe away oily residue that may be on the surface of post earring backs and ring bases.

How to Make Stud Earrings or a Ring

1. Create an indentation in the back of the finished, unbaked miniature.

2. Use a needle tool to rough up the clay inside the indentation to create extra surface area.

3. After your piece is baked and cooled, rub the front of the earring pad against sandpaper to remove the finish.

4. Dip a cotton swab in rubbing alcohol and clean off the sanded pad of the ear post and the indentation on the miniature.

5. Add a large drop of cyanoacrylate glue to the front of the earring pad, then press the pad firmly into place in the back of the earring. A bit of glue may squeeze out around the edge of your post. Scrape it off with the end of a toothpick—not your fingers! Cyanoacrylate glue is not a substance you want on your skin.

6. Set the piece aside for several hours to set. Most glue will be dry to the touch in less than an hour but needs a full day or so to completely set. We recommend waiting until the pieces are fully set before you wear them.

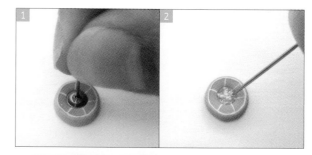
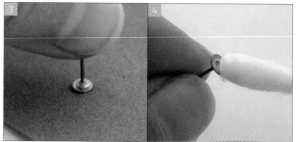
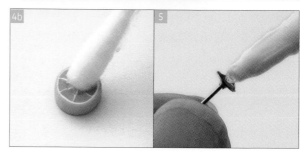

3

Fresh Fruit

· ·

We love fresh fruits—for their wonderful flavor, their bright, happy colors, and the memories they bring back. As kids, we spent at least an entire day every autumn picking apples with our family. We were fascinated by the banana tree that grew outside our grandma's window. Dad had fantastic gardens, and we always loved to pick the enormous watermelons. Lemons remind us of summers spent trying our hand at lemonade stands.

This chapter introduces basic concepts in sculpture, color mixing, and creating texture, and a very cool technique called caning.

· ·

Crisp Red Apple

JESSICA ✳ Every autumn, our family used to go apple picking. We'd weave through the orchards in the crisp fall air, trying an apple from each tree to make sure each one had truly worthy fruits. Mom made futile attempts to be the voice of moderation while Dad always insisted on "just one more box." After we lugged our apples to the car, we would drink fresh cider and plot how many pies we'd be able to make from our haul. We both still love to pick apples every fall—I'm a Fuji fiend; Susan's partial to Granny Smith.

This recipe is all about basic sculpture techniques. We also cover two kinds of color mixing: thorough and marbling. The headpin serves a dual purpose: it turns the apple into a charm, and also reinforces the delicate stem so it won't break off while you're out apple picking in your new earrings.

YIELD: 1 APPLE

INGREDIENTS

APPLE:

¼" (6.4 mm) ball cadmium red clay

¼" (6.4mm) ball alizarin crimson clay

STEM:

⅛" (3.2 mm) ball ecru clay

¹⁄₁₆" (1.6 mm) ball burnt sienna clay

LEAF:

⅛" (3.2 mm) ball green clay
¹⁄₁₆" (1.6 mm) ball alizarin crimson clay

Headpin
Large double-ball stylus
Safety pin

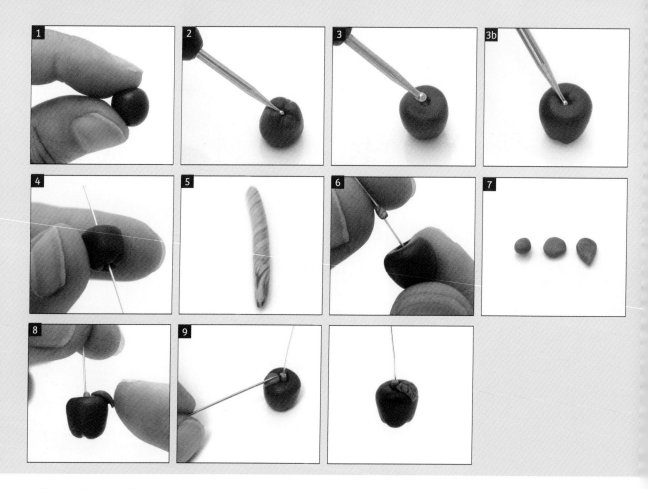

1. Thoroughly mix the two apple red clays. Roll into a smooth ball the size of a large pea. Gently flatten the center of the top, then lightly pinch the sides to make the bottom slightly narrower than the top.

2. Use the small side of a double-ball stylus (or the end of a toothpick) to create an "X" in the bottom.

Don't worry about making it perfect—real apples are uneven! Roll the stylus gently so the edges of the "X" are slightly rounded, just like the "feet" on a Red Delicious apple.

3. Use the larger side of the double-ball stylus to create a shallow indentation in the center of the top.

Use the side of the stylus to round and smooth the edge.

4. Insert a headpin through the center of the "X", making sure it comes out through the middle of the indentation on top. The bottom of the headpin should be flush with the bottom of the apple. Wash your hands and tile to remove any pink.

5. To make the stem, marble the ecru and the dark brown together (see page 21).

6. Make a short cylinder from the marbled clay and slide it onto a headpin. The trick is to give the clay cylinder a small, gentle twist, then use the back of your fingernail to push down the stem. If you have cooler hands, you can use your fingertips instead. The stem will likely get distorted. That's okay—you can fix it once it is resting within the indentation of the apple.

7. To make the leaf, mix the green and alizarin crimson. Roll the clays into a smooth ball, then flatten the ball into a thick pancake. Pinch one side of the pancake between your thumb and forefinger to create a teardrop shape.

8. Add the leaf to the apple. The rounded side goes next to the stem while the pointed tip curves down around the surface of the apple. Be sure the entire leaf lies on the surface of your apple to make it nice and sturdy.

9. Use a safety pin or your fingernail to impress a line down the center of the leaf, then veins along each side. This will make your leaf look more realistic and further bond it to the apple.

10. Bake for 15 minutes at 275° F (135° C).

To Make Apple Earrings

1. Create two matching apples.

2. Finish the headpins in the apples into closed, wrapped loops (see page 35).

3. Add a 4mm green Czech glass bead above each apple.

4. Add the earrings to ear wires of your choice.

Sweet Banana

SUSAN ✳ I've always felt bananas were the most unique of the "everyday" fruits, full of subtle contradictions. They're not juicy, but not dry either. They have seeds, but none you really notice. They're chewy and soft, but not too delicate. This soft yet tough-skinned fruit also reminds me of our grandmother—possibly for her similar qualities, but mostly for visits under the fabulous banana tree that grew outside her Southern California home. I don't think the tree ever bore much edible fruit, but that didn't stop us from enjoying the small urban jungle its broad leaves created. It was our own little haven while our grandmother watched us from her front steps.

While this recipe is for only one charm, its quick, simple construction may inspire you to create a whole bunch. After all, what better way to wear your daily dose of potassium than with a beaded banana bracelet?

YIELD: 1 BANANA

INGREDIENTS

BANANA:

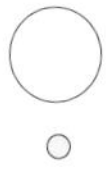

¼" (6.4 mm) ball white clay

$^1/_{16}$" (1.6 mm) ball cadmium yellow clay

PEEL:

$^5/_{16}$" (8 mm) ball cadmium yellow clay

Headpin

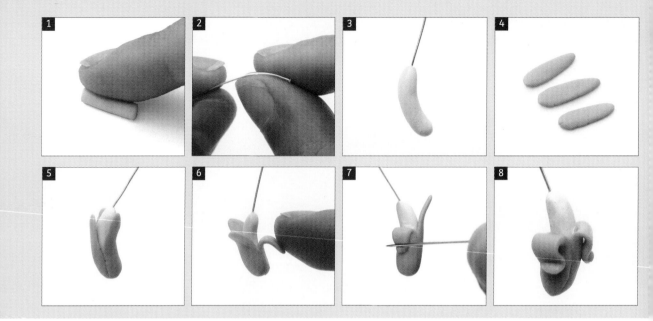

1. Thoroughly mix the smaller ball of yellow with the ball of white clay. On a clean work surface, roll the off-white clay into a small cylinder, roughly ½" (13 mm) long and less than ⅛" (3.2 mm) in diameter.

2. Gently curve the head end of a headpin around your fingertip.

3. Slide the off-white cylinder onto the headpin so the clay follows the curve of the pin. The headpin will stick out of the top of the banana. Gently round both ends of the cylinder.

4. To create the peel, divide the remaining yellow clay into three equal parts. Flatten each portion into an elongated oval roughly ⅝" (15.9 mm) long and no more than ¼" (6.35 mm) wide. Smooth each side and the edges.

5. Add the peel segments to the banana one at a time. Press the peel gently into the center of the bottom, then curve it upward so it adheres to the bottom half of the banana. Add all three segments so the bottom of the banana is fully covered and the top half of each peel is loose.

6. Fold down the top half of each peel to form a small "loop" as shown.

7. Press the tip of the folded peel into the bottom

half with your fingernail or a pin, forming a small crease.

8. Bake for 15 to 20 minutes at 275° F (135° C).

. . . .

To Make a Banana Bracelet

. . . .

1. Create a bunch of bananas (5 to 6 charms, or more as desired).

2. Finish the headpins in each banana into closed, wrapped loops (see page 35).

3. String the banana charms onto a bracelet with size 11 chocolate brown seed beads.

Juicy Watermelon

JESSICA ✳ Summer officially arrives for me each year when the freakishly huge watermelons show up at the market. I always buy one so enormous that it fills the entire bottom shelf of the fridge. There's absolutely nothing better on that first hot day than a fat wedge of sweet fresh watermelon after an afternoon running around the backyard playing wiffleball. And when friends and I hike out to our favorite swimming hole, we still have epic, raging watermelon seed-spitting battles.

This project introduces two new sculpting techniques: sculpting from the inside out, and combining baked and raw clay.

YIELD: 7 SLICES

INGREDIENTS

FLESH:
3/16" (4.7 mm) ball alizarin crimson clay
1/2" (12.7 mm) ball translucent clay
3/8" (9.5 mm) ball white clay

RIND:
1/4" (6.4 mm) ball Granny Smith clay
3/16" (4.7 mm) ball alizarin crimson clay
1/2" (12.7 mm) ball medium green clay

SEEDS:
1/8" (3.2 mm) ball black clay

Liquid clay
Paintbrush
Tissue or razor blade
Small double-ball stylus
7 headpins

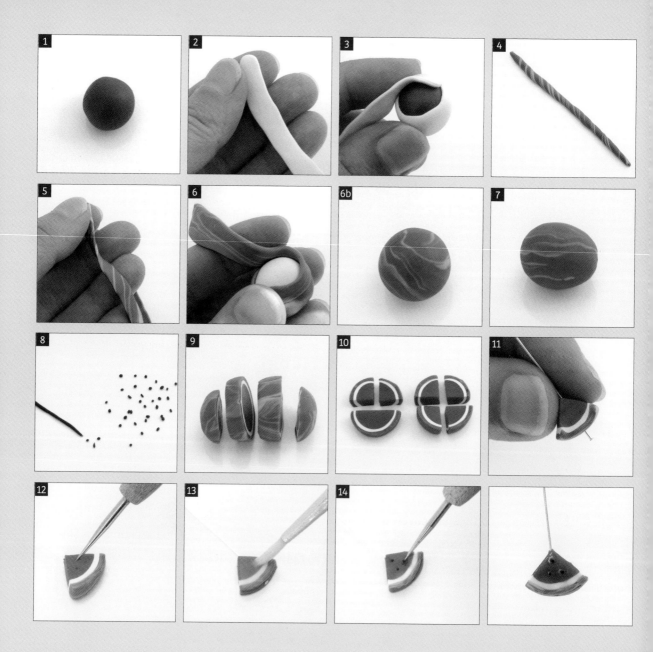

1. Thoroughly mix the alizarin crimson and translucent clays to make a uniform pink. Roll into a very smooth ball. Wash your hands before moving on to the next step.

2. Roll the white ball into a smooth sphere, then roll the sphere into a thick snake. Flatten the snake into a long strip in your hands (not on your tile).

3. Wrap the strip of white around your pink ball in layers until it is completely covered with an even, thin layer of white. Make sure there is no pink showing through. Roll the ball completely smooth to bind the white layer to the pink and even out the surface.

4. To make the watermelon rind, start by thoroughly mixing the alizarin crimson and the medium green clays to form a uniform dark green. Then marble that darker green with the light green, following the steps on page 21. You should end up with a marbled snake (leave the snake fairly fat).

5. Flatten the marbled snake into a strip.

6. Cover the white ball with a layer of green rind. It is easiest to cover the white by laying on strips of green. Once the ball is completely covered, roll it between your hands until it is very smooth.

7. Roll the watermelon between your hands to transform it from a sphere into an oblong shape that looks like a whole watermelon.

8. Let your clay cool off; the remainder of the project will be easier with cooler clay. While you are waiting, make the seeds! Roll out a long, thin snake of black clay, then pinch off tiny balls about half the size of poppy seeds. Roll the balls smooth between your fingertips. You'll need about 50 to 60 seeds in total. Bake the seeds for 5 minutes at 275° F (135° C). There's no need to quench the baked seeds; just set them aside for later.

9. Now the fun part: slicing open your watermelon! Use a tissue blade to cut your watermelon into four slices. Cut off each end, then slice the center part in half. You can use the ends to make something funky, or save the clay for another project. The two center slices of watermelon are the ones you'll use here.

10. Cut the first slice in half. Set aside one half, then cut the other half in half again. Quarter the second slice. You'll have a total of seven slices: one half slice and six quarter slices.

11. Insert a headpin into each slice, as shown. The heads should be flush with the rinds.

12. Use the small side of a double-ball stylus to create several small indentations on both sides of the pink parts. These will hold your seeds.

13. Transfer your watermelon slices to a parchment paper–covered baking tile. Paint a thin layer of

liquid clay over the pink parts of your watermelons. The liquid clay should settle into the seed indentations, making them look a tiny bit whiter than the surrounding surface.

14. Use the tip of a stylus to press one seed into each indentation.

15. Bake for 15 minutes at 275° F (135° C). The liquid clay should be translucent after quenching.

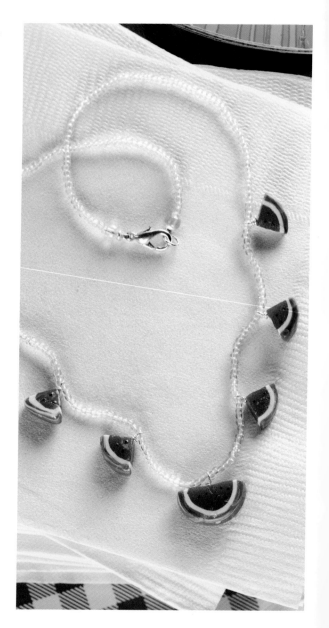

To Make a Watermelon Necklace

1. Wrap the headpin in each of your watermelons into a closed, wrapped loop (see page 35).

2. String the watermelons onto a necklace with pale pink size 11 seed beads, adding the larger slice as the central charm.

Old-Fashioned Lemonade

YIELD: 4 LARGE GLASSES OF LEMONADE

This recipe makes a small pitcher of fresh lemonade—perfect for a backyard drink in mid-summer or a refreshing reminder of summer on a cold day.

When we were kids we would set up a stand and sell our lemonade—and use our profits to buy some of life's essentials, such as jelly bracelets and fluorescent nail polish.

INGREDIENTS

1 cup (240 ml) fresh-squeezed lemon juice
(about 4 lemons)

8 tablespoons (120 ml) granulated sugar

4 cups (950 ml) ice water

1 tray ice cubes

Sliced strawberries or fresh mint
for garnish

DIRECTIONS: Warm up the lemon juice over a very low heat, and mix in the sugar until it is entirely dissolved (the heat helps the sugar dissolve.) Mix in the ice water, and add the ice cubes and garnish. Enjoy!

Lemon Slices

SUSAN ✳ Lemons for me are primarily a great accent to already delicious foods—used to dress up a simple grilled fish, or to give some tang to a strawberry pie. While I will occasionally enjoy a small wedge of lemon independently, in its purest form, my favorite way to have lemon is in freshly squeezed lemonade. As someone who doesn't usually drink soda, the tangy-sweet drink is always a refreshing afternoon pick-me-up or the perfect complement to a summer backyard gathering.

This recipe introduces caning, or MILLEFIORI. Similar to rolling sushi and then slicing it, a design is created horizontally within the cane , so when you slice the cane, the design appears on the face of each slice. This recipe also shows you how to make post earrings, which require slightly different sculpting and finishing techniques.

YIELD: 2 SLICES, PLUS EXTRA LEMON CANE FOR OTHER PROJECTS

INGREDIENTS

PULP:

¼" (6.4 mm) ball cadmium yellow clay

⅝" (16 mm) ball translucent clay

RIND:

½" (12.7 mm) ball cadmium yellow clay

PITH:

½" (12.7 mm) ball white clay

⁷⁄₁₆" (11 mm) ball white clay

Tissue or razor blade

Embroidery needle

2 earring posts

Sandpaper (220 grit)

Cyanoacrylate glue

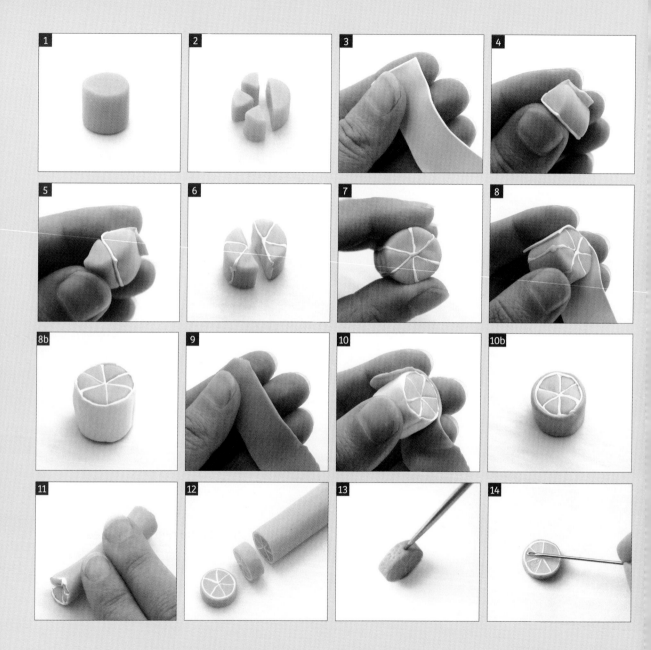

1. Thoroughly mix the small ball of yellow and the translucent clays for a bright lemony yellow. Roll into a smooth cylinder about $5/8$" (16 mm) diameter and $5/8$" (16 mm) tall. Pinch the edges to create a sharp corner from the sides to the top.

2. With a tissue blade, carefully cut the cylinder in half lengthwise, then cut each half into three equal segments. The six segments do not have to be perfectly matched, but should be similar in size.

3. In your hands (not on your tile), flatten the smaller ball of white clay into a long, thin sheet about $2^{1/4}$" (57 mm) long and $3/4$" (19 mm) wide. Cut the sheet into thirds, making three squares.

4. Align one white piece with the inner flat edges of one wedge, and wrap the white piece around, leaving the rounded side uncovered. Trim any excess clay.

5. Align an adjoining wedge of yellow as shown. The white clay should separate the two pieces, just as the membrane in a real lemon separates each wedge of pulp. Add a third wedge to form a semicircle.

6. Repeat step 5 with the second half of your pulp segments. Add the remaining sheet of white clay on the face of the second semicircle, so there is pith separating all six wedges.

7. Gently press the two halves together.

8. Flatten the remaining white clay into a thin sheet, as in step 3. Wrap the white sheet around your cylinder. Trim off any excess white hanging over the ends.

9. In your hands, flatten the remaining yellow clay into a thin rectangular sheet.

10. Wrap the sheet of yellow clay around your cylinder. Cut off any excess yellow hanging over the ends and gently smooth the sides.

11. To reduce your cane, use your fingers to gently roll it back and forth across your tile. Apply even, gentle pressure, and roll all parts of the cane so the design inside does not become distorted. Don't worry if the ends become disfigured. You can reduce the cane as small as you'd like, but a good diameter for stud earrings and beads is between $3/8$" (9.5 mm) and $1/4$" (6.4 mm).

12. If your clay is very warm, let it cool. Your slices will be much cleaner with cooler clay. Then, slice your cane in half with a tissue blade. Set aside half for future projects, such as lemon beads or tiny accents for cakes or cupcakes. Cut two slices from the other half, each about $1/8$" (3.2 mm) thick.

13. To add texture to the rind, use a needle tool to stipple around the entire outer bright yellow edge.

14. To add a pulpy texture to each slice, press the eye of an embroidery needle into the translucent

  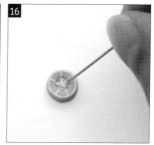

portion of your lemon. Work from the outside of each segment inward, moving in a circular pattern until you've created texture inside all six translucent segments.

15. Move your lemon slices to a baking tile and turn them over so the front, textured side is facing down. Press the flat end of a stud earring post gently into the center of each slice to create an indentation.

16. With a straight pin or needle tool, rough up the inside of the indentation to create extra surface area for the glue to bond to when you finish your earrings.

17. Bake for 15 minutes at 275° F (135° C).

To Make Lemon Stud Earrings

1. Gently clean the back of the lemon slices with a cotton swab dipped in rubbing alcohol.

2. Rub the front of the earring posts against a piece of sandpaper to rough up the surfaces of the metal.

3. Add a small drop of cyanoacrylate glue to the post earring and press it into the indent on the back of the lemon slices (see page 47). Let dry for 24 hours.

The Wide World of Citrus

Lemons not your style? No worries, this recipe can also be used to create limes, oranges, grapefruits, and even blood oranges. The changes below are all you need to adjust for the citrus of your choice.

GRAPEFRUITS: Use orange-yellow clay for the outer rind ($^1/_8$" (3.2 mm) ball of orange and $^1/_4$" (6.4 mm) ball of yellow), then make a small mix of red and orange to add into the translucent for the pulp. Since the red-orange is a deeper hue, you may want to add either more translucent or less red-orange than the recipe calls for, until the correct pinkish hue is created. If making a multicitrus piece, you may also want to reduce the cane closer to $^3/_8$"(9.5 mm) diameter or wider, since grapefruits are larger than other citrus fruits.

BLOOD ORANGES: Use the orange-yellow mixture from the grapefruit for the outer rind, and combine a bit of red and purple with the translucent for the pulp.

LIMES: Replace both balls of yellow with yellow-green clay, made by mixing half green and half yellow.

ORANGES: Replace both balls of yellow with yellow-orange clay, made by mixing $^1/_8$" (3.2 mm) ball of yellow and $^1/_4$" (6.4 mm) ball of orange.

*

4

Morning Favorites

Start your day off right! We included our favorite breakfast foods here: waffles with butter and syrup, cinnamon rolls, and a blue plate full of bacon and eggs. Of course, no breakfast is complete without (as Dolly Parton said), a nice big "cup of ambition," so we've also included a coffee mug recipe!

In this chapter, we'll cover several new techniques, from reinforcing delicate pieces of clay with wire to creating a square cane. We'll also use some new materials, including soft pastels and allspice, as well as show you a few more uses for liquid clay.

Mug o'Java

SUSAN ✳ Our daily brew is both an essential part of our morning routine and our beverage of choice for carefree conversation after a hearty meal. Although we've used a plain white mug for the earrings here, our favorite mugs definitely have their own flair. Jessica's is cow-like, complete with an udder; and mine is a classic yard sale find that proclaims Bingo players are "hot stuff." We encourage you to replace the white clay with your favorite color, or add text to create a personalized mug.

This recipe builds on what you've already learned about using wire to reinforce delicate components.

YIELD: 1 COFFEE MUG

INGREDIENTS

MUG:
3/8" (9.5 mm) ball white clay
1/4" (6.4 mm) ball pearl clay

COFFEE:
1/4" (6.4 mm) ball black clay
3/16" (4.7 mm) ball burnt sienna clay

3/4" length of 24-gauge wire
Headpin
Needle-nose pliers
Utility knife

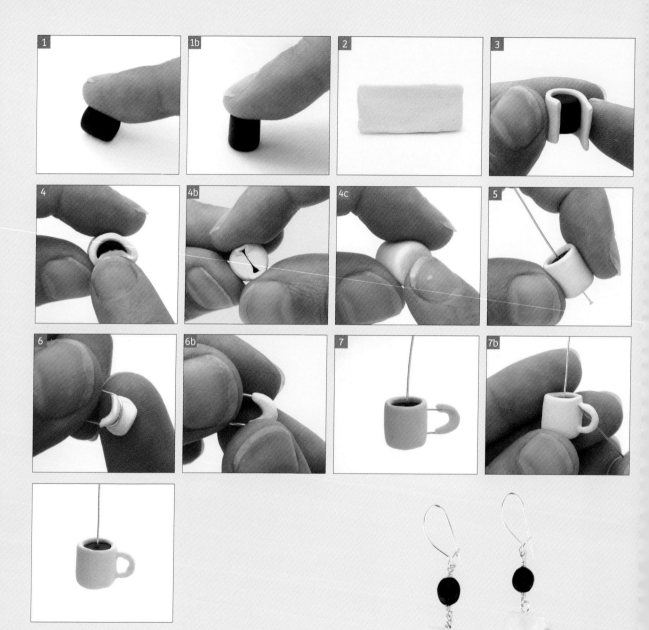

1. To make the coffee, thoroughly mix the brown and black clays. Roll the coffee mix into a cylinder about ¼" (12.7 mm) in diameter. Stand the cylinder upright and gently press down to flatten the ends. The cylinder should be about ³/₈" (9.5 mm) tall. Wash your hands and tile to remove any dark brown.

2. Mix the white and pearl clays until you have an even, faintly sparkly white. Pinch off a small (about ¹/₈" or 3.2 mm) ball and set it aside. In your hands, flatten the remaining white clay into a 1" x ³/₄" rectangle (25.4 x 19 mm).

3. Place the coffee cylinder on its side on the white rectangle so there is an overlap of less than ¹/₈" (3.18 mm) on one edge and about ¼" (6.35 mm) on the other. Roll the white rectangle around the cylinder until both sides of the rectangle meet. Smooth the mug until it looks seamless.

4. Fold the overlapping white clay onto the bottom of the cylinder, one half at a time. Then pinch together the excess clay to fully cover the bottom. Smooth the bottom surface so it sits flat against your tile.

5. Insert a headpin through the center of the mug.

6. Center a ³/₄" (19 mm) piece of 24-gauge wire around the base of your pliers and bend the wire around one side, forming a "U." Flatten the remaining white clay into a pancake and fold it around the curve of the wire. Pinch the clay closed around the wire. Only the back half of the wire should be coated; the ends should remain exposed.

7. Align the handle against the mug and push the wire ends in until the handle touches the mug's side. Use a pin or other small tool to smooth the joints between the handle and mug, also smoothing and evening out the handle.

8. Bake for 15 minutes at 275° F (135° C).

. . . .

To Make Coffee Mug Earrings
. . . .

1. Create two matching mugs and two coffee bean charms (see sidebar on next page).

2. Finish the headpins in the coffee mugs into closed, wrapped loops (see page 35).

3. Add a bean charm onto a double-sided loop (see page 36) above each coffee mug as if it were a regular accent bead.

4. Finish the earrings on ear wires of your choice.

Coffee Beans

Here's how to make coffee beans, which work as cute accents on coffee mug earrings, or as beads on a necklace or bracelet.

INGREDIENTS

- ⅛" (3.2 mm) ball burnt sienna clay
- ⅛" (3.2 mm) ball black clay

1. Mix the brown and black clays. Flatten the clay into a small oval and place it against your work surface. Round the top of the oval to create a bean shape.

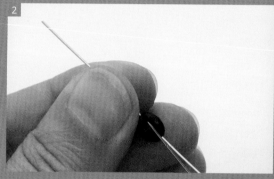

2. Slide the bean onto a headpin or scrap piece of wire. Rotate the bean a few times to loosen the hole.

3. With the edge of a straight pin, indent the center of the flat side with a vertical line. Indent two small lines on each side to form an abstract "X" shape.

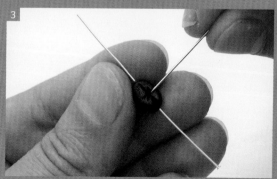

4. Bake for 15 minutes at 275° F (135° C).

Sunday Morning Cinnamon Rolls

YIELD: 6 TO 8 ROLLS

This recipe makes some small (but edible!) cinnamon rolls from a simple pastry dough—not quite the traditional breakfast version, but a nice midmorning snack. Our mom used to make these from the leftovers of pie crust dough for a small, sweet snack.

INGREDIENTS

For the dough:

1/2 cup (120 ml) unbleached flour

1/2 cup (120 ml) plus 1 tablespoon (15 ml) cake flour

1/8 teaspoon (.63 ml) baking powder

1/8 teaspoon (.63 ml) salt

4 1/2 tablespoons (67.5 ml) shortening

1 tablespoon (15 ml) butter

1/2 tablespoon (7.5 ml) vinegar

3 to 4 tablespoons (45 to 60 ml) ice water

For the cinnamon filling:

1/2 tablespoon (7.5 ml) sugar

1/4 teaspoon (1.3 ml) cinnamon

2 tablespoons (30 ml) butter, melted

DIRECTIONS: Mix together the flour, cake flour, baking powder, and salt in a large mixing bowl. Cut in the shortening and butter, either with a pastry mixer or with two butter knives, until the mixture is even and mealy—without any large clumps of shortening remaining. Stir in the vinegar, and add the ice water one tablespoon at a time, until the dough sticks together firmly.

Preheat the oven to 375° F (190° C). Roll the dough out into a large rectangle onto a lightly floured surface. Roll as thin as possible, or less than 1/4"(6.4 mm) thick. Cut the rectangle into 3 or 4 pieces lengthwise, and then cut each strip diagonally into 2 elongated triangles.

Stir in the sugar and cinnamon with the melted butter, then mix thoroughly. Brush the cinnamon-sugar mixture onto one side of each triangle, and roll the dough from the thicker edge into a coil. Place the finished rolls on a baking sheet, bake for 10 to 12 minutes or until lightly browned.

Glazed Cinnamon Roll

JESSICA ✳ Who can resist a fresh cinnamon roll? There's the buttery, yeasty sweet bread . . . the spicy cinnamon . . . the warm vanilla icing dribbling just a bit onto your hands. And if that weren't enough, cinnamon rolls are also a ton of fun to eat, peeled in chunks from the crispy outside to the soft center. Each Saturday morning, as soon as we've set up our booth at the farmer's market, I scurry over to the baker's booth to get my fresh cinnamon roll. By 7 a.m. I'm fortified and ready to laugh with customers.

This project uses liquid clay in a new way: we'll tint it with oil pastel and mix in a little mica powder so it will look just like real ooey-gooey frosting. We'll also use ground allspice to create a realistic cinnamon-sugar filling. While you're creating it, this project smells nearly as good as the real thing!

YIELD: 1 ROLL

INGREDIENTS

ROLL:
3/8" (9.5 mm) ball ecru clay

FILLING:
1/8" (3.2 mm) ball burnt sienna clay
1/4" (6.4 mm) ball translucent clay

Ground allspice
Raw sienna soft pastel
White oil pastel
Liquid clay
Fine pearl mica powder
Paintbrush
Toothpick
Headpin

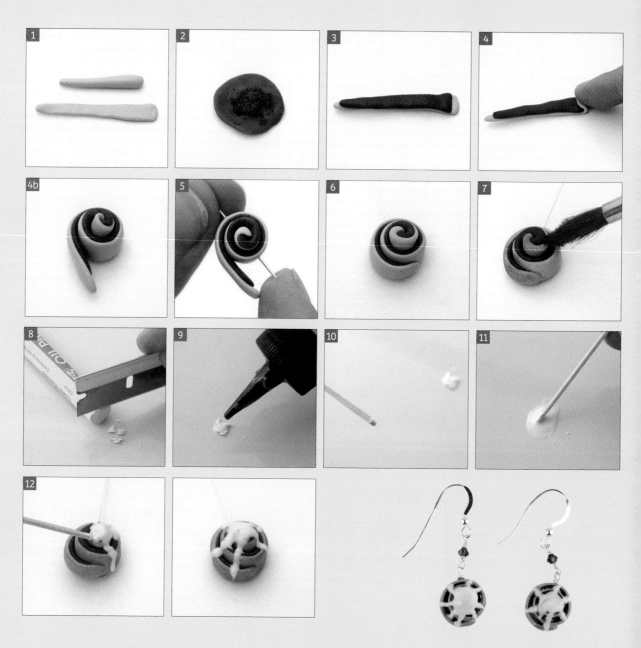

1. Roll the ecru clay into a smooth ball, then roll it into a thick, tapered log about twice as thick at one end (shown at top). Flatten the log in your hands into an elongated triangle about 2" (51 mm) long (shown at bottom).

2. Thoroughly mix the burnt sienna and translucent clays with the ground allspice to create a spicy brown mixture for the filling.

3. Similarly to step 1, roll out and then flatten the filling into an elongated triangle about ½" (3.18 mm) shorter than the ecru on either end. Press the filling onto the ecru to bind the two layers together.

4. Curl the thick end of the ecru over the filling. Continue rolling the two layers together from the thick side to the thin. Stop when you have about ½" (13 mm) remaining.

5. Insert a headpin through the center of the partially unrolled side and out the opposite side.

6. Finish rolling the cinnamon roll closed so the thin end covers the head of the headpin. Press the end to secure it to the inner layers.

7. Rub the raw sienna pastel against a scrap piece of paper until a small pile of powder forms. With a paintbrush, dab an uneven layer of powder over the ecru parts to make the roll look baked. Wash your hands, the paintbrush, and your tile before moving on.

8. To make the icing, use a razor blade to shave a few pieces of white oil pastel onto your tile.

9. Add several drops of liquid clay.

10. Add a tiny amount of pearl mica powder.

11. Thoroughly mix with a toothpick until no lumps remain. The icing should be uniformly white and a tad sparkly. It's now ready to drizzle!

12. Use a toothpick to drizzle icing on top of the roll. Add as much or as little as you'd like! Real cinnamon rolls usually have the most in the center and a few dribbles down the sides.

13. Bake for 15 minutes at 275° F (135° C).

To Make Cinnamon Roll Earrings

1. Make two matching cinnamon roll charms.

2. Finish the headpins in the cinnamon rolls into closed, wrapped loops (see page 35).

3. Wrap a dark topaz 3mm crystal as an accent above each cinnamon roll (see page 36). Finish on ear wires of your choice.

Golden Waffle Drizzled with Syrup

SUSAN ✻ Ah, waffles, the staple of every Sunday brunch buffet. Forget perfectly prepared yogurt parfaits, fruit salad, or the omelette station—the custom waffle stand always offers the tastiest morning treat, no matter what my mood may be. Whether loading up on a variety of fruit compotes, nuts, or whipped cream, I always make sure to fill each perfectly crisped and geometric nook to its brim with extra sweetness.

This recipe makes one deliciously adorable waffle charm, complete with melting butter and a hefty drizzle of maple syrup.

YIELD: 1 WAFFLE

INGREDIENTS

WAFFLE:

³/₈" (9.5 mm) ball ecru clay

BUTTER:

○ ¹/₁₆" (1.6 mm) ball cadmium yellow clay
○ ¹/₁₆" (1.6 mm) ball ivory clay

Raw sienna soft pastel

Light brown oil pastel

Reddish brown oil pastel

Liquid clay

Square toothpick

Sandpaper

Paintbrush

Scrap paper

Utility knife or razor blade

Headpin

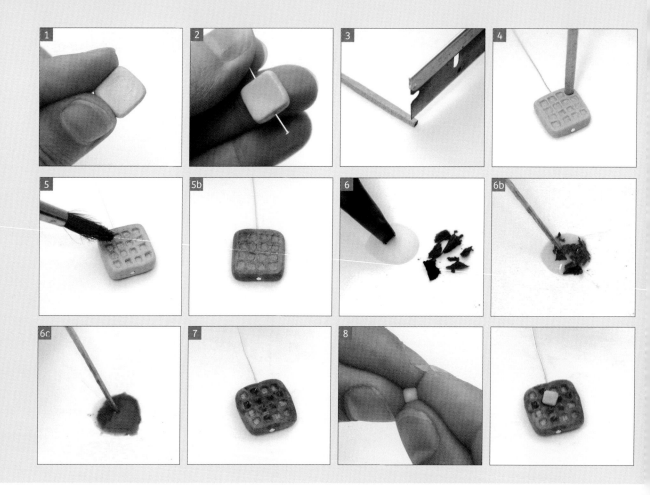

1. Flatten the ball of ecru clay into a pancake and form into a square just under ½" (13 mm) wide and ⅛" (3.2 mm) thick. Press the sides and edges against your work surface to make them smooth and defined.

2. Insert a headpin through the middle of one side.

3. To create a waffle texture, first make a square tool. Use a razor blade or utility knife to cut the toothpick where it is most perfectly square. If the cut end is a bit rough, sand it to make a flat, even square.

4. Use the square end of the toothpick to create a

4 x 4" grid of evenly spaced indentations on your waffle, leaving a little space between the top and side edges. Flip over the waffle and create a matching grid on the back, being gentle to avoid undoing the impressions on the first side. As you do this, your square will get a little wider and taller but should still maintain an even square shape.

5. Rub the raw sienna pastel against a scrap piece of paper until a small pile of powder forms. With a paintbrush, dab a small amount on the waffle. Get both sides and each edge. Wash your hands, the paintbrush, and your tile before moving on.

6. To create maple syrup, use a knife or razor blade to shave a few pieces of the light brown and reddish brown oil pastels onto your clean tile. You'll want slightly more light brown than reddish brown flakes. Add a few drops of liquid clay, then use a fresh toothpick to mix. The finished mix should be an even warm brown without any chunks.

7. Use a clean paintbrush to paint the syrup onto the waffle, working from the middle outward. We recommend putting a good amount in the center, then painting a small amount over each edge, like a cross.

8. To make butter, thoroughly mix the ivory and yellow clays. Flatten the small ball into a pancake, and form into a small square between your thumbs and forefingers. Then add the pat of butter to the middle of the syrup. Press gently to adhere it to the waffle surface.

9. Bake at 275° F (135° C) for 15 minutes.

. . . .

To Make a Waffle Necklace
. . . .

1. Finish the headpin into a closed, wrapped loop (see page 35).

2. Add a jump ring or spring ring onto the wrapped loop, and add to a finished necklace chain. Your new brunch accessory is now ready to gobble up compliments!

Bacon and Eggs

JESSICA ✳ We grew up with a mother who believed in healthy, low-fat cooking, so bacon was a rare treat. This recipe pays homage not only to the sizzling goodness of bacon and eggs, but also to a classic Partain family story.

One morning when I was about five years old I awoke to the heavenly aroma of bacon wafting up from the kitchen downstairs. I leaped out of bed and ran to the top of the stairs. "Wait a minute," I told myself, "I could get downstairs faster if I fly." So, I launched myself off the top step. Gravity, sadly, intervened and I proceeded to tumble all the way down. Mom came running over and asked in a panicked voice whether I was okay. I simply replied, "Baaaacon."

This project has two special features. We'll use liquid clay extensively—both as an adhesive and to reinforce the delicate bacon. We'll also use a variation on caning to create the bacon.

YIELD: 1 PLATE OF BACON AND EGGS

INGREDIENTS

PLATE:
$3/16$" (4.7 mm) ball turquoise clay
$3/8$" (9.5 mm) ball white clay

EGG:
$1/8$" (3.2 mm) ball cadmium yellow clay
$3/16$" (4.7 mm) ball white clay

BACON:
$1/8$" (3.2 mm) ball alizarin crimson clay
$1/4$" (6.4 mm) ball raw sienna clay
$1/4$" (6.4 mm) ball ivory clay

Liquid clay
Double-ball stylus
Paintbrush
Ring base
Needle tool
Cyanoacrylate glue
Rubbing alcohol
Sandpaper (220 grit)

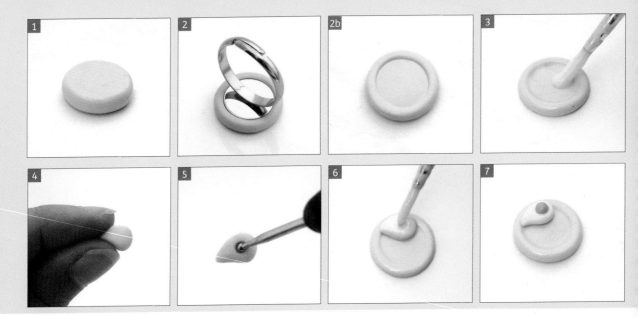

1. Thoroughly mix the turquoise and larger ball of white clays to create a uniform pale blue. Make a smooth sphere, then flatten it into a thick pancake a little more than ½" (13 mm) in diameter.

2. Press the flat pad of the ring base into the center of the pancake to create an indentation. Flip over the pancake and create another indentation. Choose the side you prefer; this will be the front of your plate. The other side will have a guideline for where to glue your ring base.

3. Paint a thin layer of liquid clay over the front of the plate. You don't need to paint the back.

4. To make the egg, roll the small ball of white clay very smooth, then flatten it into a pancake. Gently pinch one side to create a curved teardrop shape.

5. Use the larger side of a double-ball stylus to create a shallow indentation in the round part of your egg white.

6. Press the egg white gently onto the plate. Add a tiny drop of liquid clay into the indentation.

7. To make the yolk, roll the yellow clay into a very smooth ball, then press it into place in the indentation. Use your paintbrush to smooth out any liquid clay that squishes out from between the white and the yolk.

8. Prepare two pieces of bacon (see sidebar on opposite page).

Making Bacon

Bacon is an easy cane to create. It is just four layers of clay stacked and reduced to the correct size.

1. Thoroughly mix the alizarin crimson and raw sienna clays. Roll into a smooth ball, then flatten into a pancake. Square off the edges, making a short rectangle. Repeat with the ivory clay, so you have two rectangles the same size: one for the meat, one for the fat.

2. Stack the fat on top of the meat. Press gently and evenly to adhere the two layers together.

3. Slice the rectangle in half crossways to make two equal squares. Stack the squares on top of one another, making sure the sequence is: meat, fat, meat, fat.

4. Press the square evenly until it is about ¼"– ⅓" the height of the original stack, as shown. Your bacon cane should be a rectangle again.

5. Use a tissue blade to cut a thick slice of bacon from the shorter side of your cane, and discard that first slice. Slice two more thick pieces of bacon.

6. Flatten each slice of bacon between your fingertips until it is about twice the length of the original slice. The width of it should remain the same.

7. Gently push up and down on the slice of bacon to create a wavy surface.

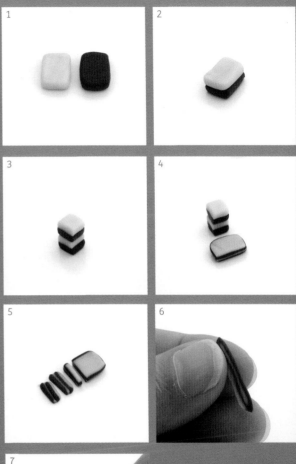

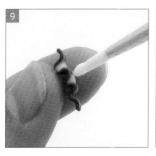

9. Reinforce the bacon by painting a thick layer of liquid clay underneath each arch, so the liquid clay is even with the bottom of the bacon. Add the two pieces of bacon to your plate.

10. Bake for 15 minutes at 275° F (135° C). The liquid clay should be translucent after quenching, but if it is still a bit cloudy, bake the plate again for another 15 minutes.

To Make a Bacon and Eggs Ring

1. Use a needle tool to gently carve an uneven surface all over the back of your baked plate, where your ring base will be glued. This will create more surface area for the glue to grab onto and will make your ring sturdier.

2. Rub the pad of your ring base over coarse sandpaper to rough it up.

3. Use a cotton swab dipped in rubbing alcohol to wash any remaining surface oils off the back of your plate and the pad of your ring base. Let both thoroughly dry.

4. Add a thin layer of cyanoacrylate glue to the pad of the ring base, then press it into the back of your plate of bacon and eggs. Let dry until set (24 hours is ideal).

5. If you'd like to glaze your ring, paint a thin layer of glaze after the glue has completely set.

Bacon, Chives, and Cheddar Omelette YIELD: 1 OMELETTE

Our family has always been big on brunch. As adults, we both still love to go out for a lazy Sunday breakfast at one of our favorite local places. It's always a tough choice between the French toast and the specialty omlettes. Here is a delicious omlette that will make every morning feel like a weekend breakfast!

INGREDIENTS

2 eggs

2 tablespoons (30 ml) milk

1 slice cooked bacon (or veggie bacon), crumbled

1 tablespoon (15 ml) chopped fresh chives

4 tablespoons (60 ml) shredded sharp cheddar

1 tablespoon (15 ml) olive oil

Salt and fresh ground pepper to taste

DIRECTIONS:

Whisk together the eggs and milk. Mix in the bacon and chives.

Heat an 8" (203 ml) cast iron (or nonstick) skillet to medium hot, then add the oil. Add the egg mixture, then cover the skillet with a lid. This will steam the top part of the omelette and make it fluffy.

When the omlette is cooked, add the cheese to half of it, then fold the other half of the egg over to make a half-moon.

Sprinkle some sea salt and fresh ground pepper on top, and enjoy!

5

Savory Entrees

We love the range of flavors and textures that liven up the savory foods in our daily routines. We can't think of much that's better for a quick midday bite than a burger loaded with crisp veggies and gooey cheese from the local diner, or a platter of tangy sushi. We remember fondly our family dinners as children, when we'd create our own masterpieces on taco night or split a quick pizza on busy evenings.

This chapter features these diverse meals using equally diverse techniques, from making compound canes to various color-mixing techniques, and even baking a charm in two stages.

Make-It-Your-Way Burger

JESSICA ✳ The perfect hamburger starts with a thick, perfectly spiced hand-formed patty—mine would be an awesome veggie burger with lots of mushrooms. Add a slice of creamy cheese that melts just a bit down the side. You could stop there, or add a slice of ripe tomato and crisp lettuce. And no burger is complete (low-carb dieters notwithstanding!) without a freshly toasted sesame seed bun.

The basic steps in creating this tiny burger are exactly the same as creating a real one (without the need for a grill and lighter fluid). You can add all of your favorite toppings—perhaps you prefer a double cheeseburger, or a savory slice of onion? Or maybe you have a special sauce? Whatever your preference, add it to your tiny burgers to make them totally personalized!

YIELD: 1 BURGER

INGREDIENTS

BUN:

$1/16$" (1.6 mm) ball white clay

$1/4$" (6.4 mm) ball ecru clay

$3/8$" (9.5 mm) ball ecru clay

BURGER, CHEESE, AND TOMATO:

$1/4$" (6.4 mm) ball burnt sienna clay

$3/16$" (4.7 mm) ball cadmium yellow clay

$3/16$" (4.7 mm) ball cadmium red clay

LETTUCE:

$3/16$" (4.7 mm) ball translucent clay

$1/16$" (1.6 mm) ball light green clay

$1/8$" (3.2 mm) ball medium green clay

Raw sienna soft pastel

Double-ball stylus

Paintbrush

Headpin

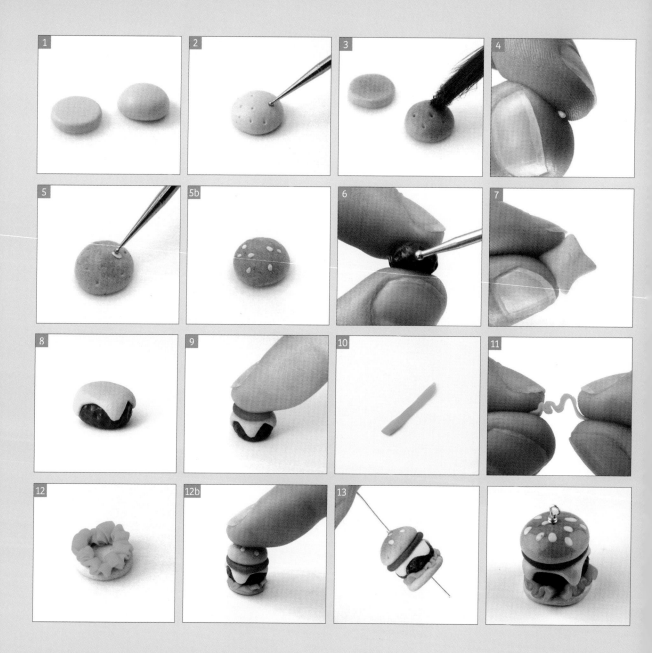

1. Start with the bun. Flatten the smaller ball of ecru clay into a pancake for the bottom half. Form the larger ball of ecru into a rounded dome for the top half.

2. Use the small side of a double-ball stylus to make several scattered indentations on the top bun.

3. Rub the raw sienna pastel against a scrap piece of paper until a small pile of powder forms. With a paintbrush dab the top of the top bun and the bottom of the bottom bun with a little of the powder to make them look toasty. Use a gentle touch so the indentations don't get pastel in them. Wash your hands, the paintbrush, and your tile before moving on.

4. Roll the white clay into a very thin snake, then cut off a ball for each indentation in the top bun—these will be your sesame seeds. Pinch each seed between your fingers to create a teardrop shape.

5. Use a stylus to place one seed into each indentation on your top bun.

6. To create the patty, flatten the ball of burnt sienna clay into a nice thick pancake a little less than 1/2" (1.3 cm) in diameter. Use a double-ball stylus to add dimpled texture all over the surface.

7. To make the cheese, flatten the ball of yellow clay into a pancake in your hands, and then pinch it between your fingertips to form a square. Each corner should remain a bit rounded, since when real cheese melts, it loses its sharp edges.

8. Add the cheese on top of the patty, gently pulling down the corners of the cheese to mimic melting.

9. Flatten the red ball into a pancake about the same diameter as your burger patty. Roll the edges of the pancake against your tile to make the edges look crisp, like a freshly sliced tomato. Add the tomato to the top of the cheese. Wash your hands to remove any red.

10. Thoroughly mix the light green and translucent clays to create a pale lettuce green. Marble together the lettuce color with the medium green clay (see page 21). Flatten into a strip about 1/8" (3.2 mm) wide.

11. Divide the green strip into three pieces. Ruffle each piece between your fingers, as shown.

12. Add all three pieces of lettuce to the bottom bun. Then add the patty, cheese, and tomato. Add the top bun, and press gently to bind all layers together.

13. Slide a headpin through the center of all layers, so the head rests flush with the bottom of the bottom bun.

14. Bake for 20 minutes at 275°F (135° C).

To Make Burger Earrings

1. Create two matching burgers.

2. Finish the headpin in each burger into a closed, wrapped loop (see page 35).

3. Add a 3mm red crystal accent on a double-sided loop (see page 36) above each burger.

4. Finish the earrings on ear wires of your choice.

Grandma's Pasta Sauce

YIELD: 4 SERVINGS

Our grandma used to make absolutely incredible Italian food, including her own pasta sauce from scratch. She used it as the sauce for all sorts of dishes. Nowadays, we like it over penne with plenty of Parmesan.

INGREDIENTS

4 large tomatoes (about 1¹/₂ pounds or .68 kilos)

4 tablespoons (60 ml) extra virgin olive oil

1 teaspoon (5 ml) sea salt

2 tablespoons (30 ml) thinly sliced fresh basil

1 tablespoon (15 ml) minced garlic

Freshly ground pepper to taste

DIRECTIONS: Bring heavily salted water to a boil in a large stockpot. Blanch the tomatoes for about 30 seconds to loosen the skin, then put the tomatoes in a bowl of ice water to cool them. Peel the tomatoes and discard the skins. Smush the tomato flesh into a pulpy mass, and set aside. Discard the water from the stockpot, dry the pot, then set it over low heat. Heat the olive oil, then add the sea salt and a few grinds of fresh pepper. Add the minced garlic and stir until the garlic is fragrant, about 15 seconds (watch the garlic carefully so that it doesn't burn and go bitter). Add the crushed tomatoes, and stir thoroughly. Bring the sauce to a gentle simmer, and let it cook down until it is reduced by about half and no longer looks watery, about 30 minutes. Add the sliced basil and let it cook for about 1 minute, until bright green. Serve over freshly cooked penne with freshly grated Parmesan cheese.

This recipe also freezes well, and is better the next day, when the flavors have time to really meld.

Taco with Tasty Toppings

SUSAN ✳ As a kid, I always looked forward to taco night as my opportunity to create a culinary masterpiece. I'd skip the refried beans and load up instead with meat, tomatoes, and cheese. Sometimes I'd feel inspired to add other foods as "toppings," such as uncooked pasta, nuts, or dried fruit. My concoctions frequently received heavy criticism from parents and siblings alike, but that never stopped me from thoroughly enjoying my personalized tacos.

The taco earrings in this recipe are loaded with more traditional toppings: cheese, lettuce, tomatoes, sour cream, and chives. Just like a real taco, first we'll bake the empty shell, and then we'll pile on the toppings. For this recipe, you'll need a round oven-proof tool with a diameter of about 1/4" (6.4 mm), such as a knitting needle, a chopstick, or the metal handle of your stippling tool.

YIELD: 1 TACO

INGREDIENTS

SHELL:
3/8" (9.5 mm) ball ecru clay
5/16" (8 mm) ball cadmium yellow clay
Pinch of finely ground black pepper

MEAT:
5/16" (8 mm) ball burnt sienna clay
1/4" (6.4 mm) ball orange clay

TOPPINGS:
1/16" (1.6 mm) ball cadmium yellow clay
1/16" (1.6 mm) ball red clay
1/16" (1.6 mm) ball green clay
1/8" (3.2 mm) ball white clay

LETTUCE:
1/8" (3.2 mm) ball yellow
1/8" (3.2 mm) ball green
3/16" (4.7 mm) ball translucent

Liquid clay
Headpin
Stippling tool or straight pin
1/4" (6.4 mm) diameter oven-safe tool
Utility knife
Paintbrush

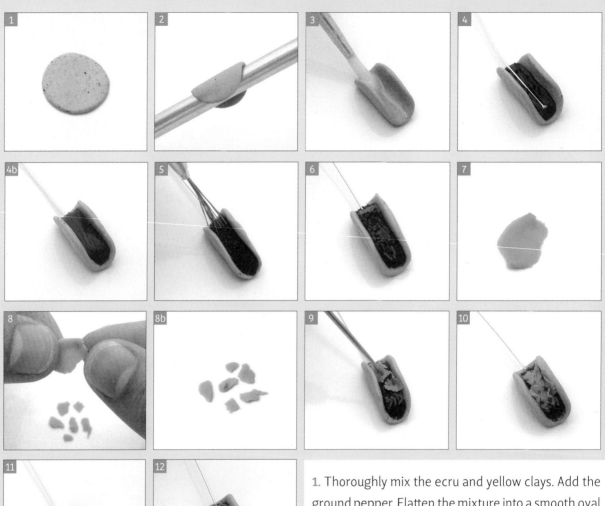

1. Thoroughly mix the ecru and yellow clays. Add the ground pepper. Flatten the mixture into a smooth oval pancake, $^3/_4$" (1.9 cm) tall and $^5/_8$" (1.6 cm) wide.

2. Fold the oval around your oven-safe tool. Bake the shell on the tool for 9 minutes at 275° F (135° C). Let cool thoroughly, then remove from the tool.

3. Paint a thin layer of liquid clay on the inside bottom of the shell.

4. Mix the brown and orange clays to get a nice spicy meat color. Divide the meat mixture in half and flatten each portion into an elongated oval, about $5/8$"(1.6 cm) long and just under $1/4$" (6.4 mm) wide. Press one brown oval to bond it with the liquid clay in the shell. Then press a headpin into the center of the meat. Add the remaining brown oval on top of the headpin.

5. Add texture to the surface of the meat with your stippling tool. Wash your hands and tile to remove any brown.

6. Roll the yellow clay into a thin snake, then cut it into about a dozen $1/8$" (3.9 mm) lengths with a utility knife. Add five to six pieces of the cheese in a criss-crossed pattern onto each end of the meat.

7. Make the lettuce. Marble the yellow, green, and translucent clays, leaving small swirls of partially-mixed color in the finished mix (see page 21). Flatten the swirly color into a very thin, unevenly edged pancake.

8. Hold one side of the pancake with one hand, and grasp an outer edge of the opposite side, pulling gently until a portion pulls apart. Repeat until the whole pancake is broken into four to five pieces. The torn pieces can be any size or shape.

9. Add four to five pieces of lettuce to the taco, arranging them so the middle of the meat is covered. Press the center of each piece with a straight pin or needle tool so each piece is firmly attached without flattening down the rough lettuce edges.

10. Roll the red clay into a small snake and cut into six small squares. Scatter these tomato pieces on top of the lettuce, pressing gently to adhere. Wash your hands to remove any red.

11. Roll the white clay into a smooth ball, then flatten one side against your tile. Press the flat side onto the middle of the lettuce.

12. Roll the green clay into a small snake, flatten it, then cut several square pieces of chives and scatter them on top of the sour cream.

13. Bake for 15 minutes at 275° F (135° C).

To Make Taco Earrings

1. Create two matching taco charms.

2. Finish the headpin in each taco into a closed, wrapped loop (see page 35).

3. Add a 3mm red crystal accent on a double-sided loop (see page 36) above each taco.

4. Finish the earrings on your ear wires of choice.

Sumptuous Sushi Platter

JESSICA ✳ When we were kids, Susan and I spent some time living in Hawaii, where sushi meant something quite different than California rolls. Our classmates would unpack bento boxes full of Spam musubi. Although the Spam version never won me over, sushi is now one of my favorite foods. I love the gorgeous presentation, with its attention to detail and the mix of rich and spicy flavors in each bite. I'm craving fresh salmon roe, perfectly ripe avocado, sweet shrimp, and fatty tuna just thinking about it!

For our sushi platter charm, the salmon is created with a simple compounded cane. You'll also learn the difference between mixing a color with white versus translucent clay and various uses for liquid clay, which is used for bonding as well as to give the platter a shiny lacquered look.

YIELD: 1 PLATTER OF SUSHI

INGREDIENTS

SUSHI:

¼" (6.4 mm) ball orange clay

¼" (6.4 mm) ball cadmium red clay

³⁄₈" (9.5 mm) ball white clay

³⁄₈" (9.5 mm) ball translucent clay

SEAWEED & RICE:

⅛" (3.2 mm) ball black clay

⅛" (3.2 mm) ball green clay

³⁄₁₆" (4.7 mm) ball white clay

WASABI:

¹⁄₁₆" (1.6 mm) ball white clay

⅛" (3.2 mm) ball Granny Smith clay

PLATTER:

½" (12.7 mm) ball black clay

2 flat wooden toothpicks

Liquid clay

Razor blade

Small double-ball stylus

Paintbrush

Headpin

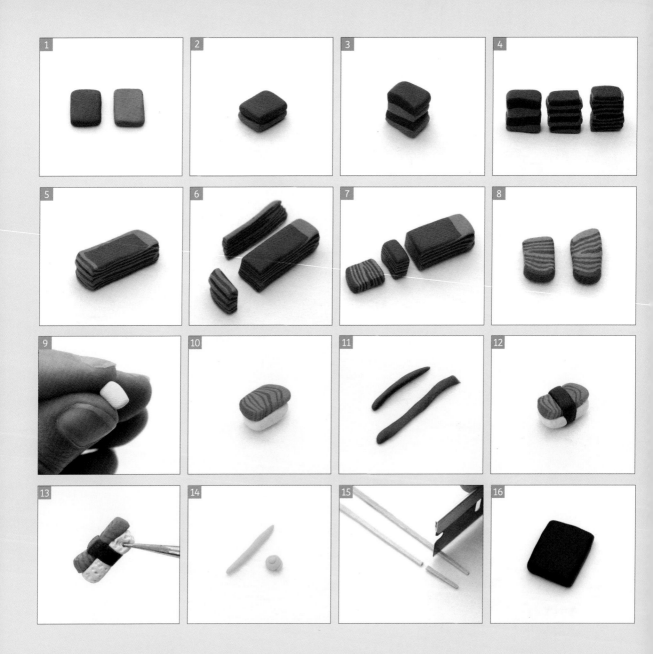

1. To create the salmon, thoroughly mix the orange and cadmium red clays. Divide the mixture in half. Mix one half with the ball of white clay, the other half with the ball of translucent clay. Flatten them into equal-sized rectangles.

2. Stack the rectangles on top of each other, then gently press together.

3. Cut the rectangle in half, then stack the two halves on top of each other, alternating pink and red layers.

4. Repeat the process of cutting the rectangle in half and compressing the whole piece two more times, until you have a total of eight layers of each color. The photo shows each step in turn.

5. Flatten your cane into a rectangle about $\frac{1}{4}$" (6.4 mm) tall and wide. Don't worry that the edges of your cane are uneven and imperfect—this is normal.

6. Use a razor blade to slice off the long imperfect edge, and one end of the cane.

7. Slice two $\frac{1}{8}$" (3.2 mm) pieces of sushi from your cleaned cane.

8. Gently flatten the two pieces and shape them into a slightly tilted rectangle, as shown. Wash your hands and tile before moving to the next step.

9. Now make the rice. Divide the small ball of white clay in half. Roll each half into a smooth ball, then flatten into a pancake. Pinch the edges between your fingertips to form a small rectangle of rice, slightly smaller than the piece of salmon.

10. Put a slice of fish on top of each rice rectangle.

11. To make the seaweed, thoroughly mix the black and green clays. Roll the seaweed into a thin snake, then flatten into a thin strip.

12. Cut the strip in half, then wrap each half around one piece of sushi.

13. Use the small tip of a double-ball stylus to create a nubby rice texture on all sides of the white piece. Set aside your finished sushi.

14. To create the wasabi, thoroughly mix the white and Granny Smith clays. Roll the ball into a thick, short snake, then spiral it into a dollop of wasabi.

15. To make the chopsticks, use a razor blade to cut off $\frac{1}{2}$" (1.3 cm) of the small end of each toothpick. Make sure the cut ends are nice and even.

16. To create the platter, roll the large ball of black clay into a very smooth ball, then flatten it into a pancake about $\frac{1}{8}$" (3.2 mm) thick. Pinch the corners to form a rectangle about $\frac{5}{8}$" x $\frac{3}{4}$" (1.6 x 1.9 cm).

17. Insert a headpin through the platter as shown and pull it through until the head is flush with the bottom of the platter.

18. Paint a thin, even layer of liquid clay all over the front and sides of your platter.

19. Place the sushi, wasabi, and chopsticks on the platter and press gently to bond them to the liquid clay.

20. Bake for 20 minutes at 275° F (135° C).

To Make a Sushi Necklace

1. Finish the headpin into a closed, wrapped loop (see page 35).

2. String the charm on a necklace with red and black size 11 seed beads.

California Rolls

Going out for sushi with a group of friends is enormously fun. Inviting friends over for a make-your-own sushi dinner is even more fun! As an added bonus, making sushi rolls will help you understand how to make polymer clay canes—they are constructed in the same way with the design only visible once you slice them!

INGREDIENTS

1½ cups (356 ml) short-grain Japanese
   sushi rice

3 cups (711 ml) water

6 tablespoons (90 ml) seasoned rice
   vinegar

2 (8.5" x 11" or 216 mm x 279 mm) sheets
   roasted seaweed (nori)

1 cup cooked crabmeat

1 avocado, peeled and sliced into strips

1 large cucumber, peeled, seeded, and
   sliced

Soy sauce

Wasabi

Pickled ginger

DIRECTIONS: Rinse the rice in a fine-mesh sieve until the water runs through clear. Add the rice and water to a medium pot and bring to a boil. Reduce the heat, cover, and let simmer for about 20 minutes, until all the water is absorbed.

Using a wooden spoon, gently turn out the rice into a wide-brimmed metal bowl. Add the seasoned rice vinegar, then use the spoon to fold the rice until the vinegar is evenly coating the rice. You always want to be folding the rice upwards to keep it fluffy. Let the rice cool.

To assemble the rolls, tear each sheet of nori in half horizontally and put a piece on a bamboo mat (or clean dishtowel). Dampen your fingers in water. Add a thin layer of rice on top of the nori; do not cover completely. Lay crabmeat, avocado, and cucumber lengthwise in the center of the rice.

Slowly fold the end of the mat closest to you over the filling and tuck it in—pull to make it tight. Remove the mat. Dip a sharp chef's knife in water, then slice the roll into 6 or 8 sections. Enjoy the sushi with soy sauce, wasabi, ginger, and a bunch of friends!

Personal Pizza

SUSAN ✳ Is it ever a bad time for pizza? My favorites are those delectable thin-crust specialties created at local hole-in-the-wall restaurants, covered with a blend of cheeses, a shake of red pepper flakes, and some oil or sauce I've never heard of. I also love how pizza is an inherently social food, with the easily swappable slices and endless variety of toppings. Of course, trying to get two sisters to agree on toppings is always a challenge. When Jess and I order pizza, we end up with two distinct halves: hers with mushrooms and olives, mine with tomatoes and green peppers.

The pizza in this recipe includes a combination of our favorites—pepperoni, green bell peppers, and black olives.

YIELD: 1 PIZZA

INGREDIENTS

CRUST:
½" (1.3 cm) ball ecru clay
¼" (6.4 mm) ball ecru clay

SAUCE:
³/₁₆" (4.7 mm) ball red clay
⅛" (3.2 mm) ball burnt sienna clay

CHEESE:
³/₁₆" (4.7 mm) ball white clay
³/₁₆" (4.7 mm) ball ivory clay

TOPPINGS:
¹/₁₆" (1.6 mm) ball black clay
¹/₁₆" (1.6 mm) ball green clay

PEPPERONI:
³/₁₆" (4.7 mm) ball ivory clay
³/₁₆" (4.7 mm) ball cadmium red clay
³/₁₆" (4.7 mm) ball alizarin crimson clay

Headpin
Raw sienna soft pastel
Tissue or razor blade
Straight pin
Paintbrush
Jump ring or spring ring
Necklace chain

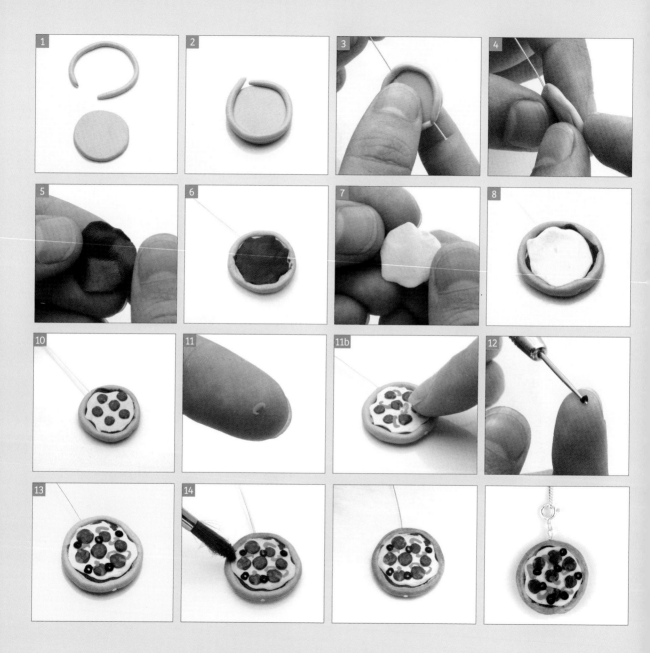

1. Flatten the larger ball of ecru clay into an even circular disk roughly $3/4$" (1.9 cm) in diameter and $1/8$" (3.2 mm) thick. Roll the smaller ball of ecru into a thin snake the same length as the circumference of your crust.

2. Press the ecru snake in place around the disk.

3. Insert a headpin through the disk until the head is flush with the outside of the crust.

4. Lightly pinch, then smooth the outside edge to erase the join between the disk and the snake.

5. Mix the red and brown clays. Flatten the mixed clay between your fingers, creating a thin, unevenly shaped pancake just over $1/2$" (1.3 cm) wide.

6. Place the red pancake inside the crust, fitting the edges mostly inside the inner crust but allowing for some overlap onto the ridge. Wash your hands and work surface to remove any red.

7. Thoroughly mix the ivory and white clays to make the mozzarella cheese. Flatten the clay into a pancake the same way you made the sauce.

8. Place the white pancake onto the pie so the uneven edge allows some red and ecru to peek out.

9. Make the pepperoni (see sidebar on next page).

10. Scatter pepperoni slices onto the cheese and gently press into place.

11. Roll the small ball of green clay into a thin snake, and cut into five to six short segments with your tissue or razor blade. Place one green segment on your finger, and curve the ends into a small, elongated "C," as shown. Press onto the pizza so that the clay is fully attached but still slightly raised above the cheese.

12. Roll the black clay into a small snake and cut into five to six small balls. Poke one ball onto the end of a straight pin, then rotate the clay until the center hole is wider than the clay edge. Repeat with each ball.

13. Gently press the small olives onto the pizza.

14. Rub the raw sienna pastel against a scrap piece of paper until a small pile of powder forms. With a paintbrush, dab some powder around the crust edge and on the bottom crust to make it look baked. Wash your hands, the paintbrush, and your tile.

15. Bake for 20 minutes at 275° F (135° C).

To Make a Pizza Necklace

1. Finish the headpin into a closed, wrapped loop (see page 35).

2. Add a jump ring or spring ring onto the wrapped loop.

3. Add the charm to a necklace chain, then wear it to the next pizza party.

Pepperoni

Curing your own miniature pepperoni is easily done by making a simple cane—much quicker than making the real thing!

1. Roll each color into two 1" (2.54 cm) long snakes, beginning with the ivory to avoid staining it red.

2. Gather the colors together in a bunch, making sure the shades are nicely intermixed.

3. Gently roll the bunch to fuse together the various snakes, then cut into fourths.

4. Align each of the quarters lengthwise and bunch them together into one thicker log.

5. Roll the stacked log into a snake just over ⅛" (3.2 mm) thick.

6. Slice off some thin pieces of your newly cured pepperoni to add onto your homemade pizza!

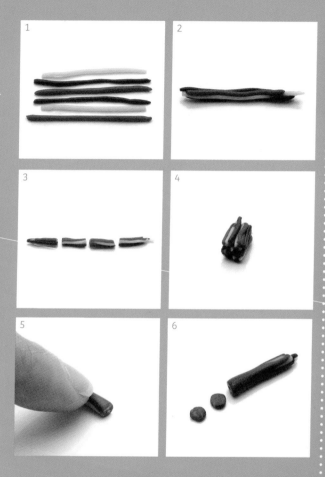

6

Sweet-Tooth Delights
and Other Treats

We come from a long line of unabashed sweet tooths. Grandma used to pull her own taffy, and to this day makes unrivaled fudge. Mom makes incredible brownies, cupcakes, and chocolate chip cookies. Dad adores ice cream and always picks up a few pints when he knows we're coming to visit. Savory snacks have a nearly equal place in our hearts. Baseball games just wouldn't be the same without big salty pretzels.

The best part of these projects is that they are customizable. The cupcake, lollipop, and ice cream can be made in your favorite flavors. The pretzel can have as much salt as you'd like, or you can even add mustard!

Yummy Cupcake

JESSICA ✳ The cupcake just might be the perfect dessert. Compact, portable, and impossible to eat in a dignified manner, cupcakes always make me happy. I'm partial to rich chocolate, or any combination of fruit with vanilla or lemon cake. And the best part? Each is a single serving, so I never feel guilty for not wanting to share.

This recipe makes a traditional chocolate cupcake with pink icing and a cherry. However, we encourage you to experiment with different cake and frosting flavors, as well as to add fun decorations to customize your cupcakes. Why not use the leftover lemon cane from the lemon recipe to add tiny lemon slices? Or make an ultraminiature candy corn to put on top for a fall cupcake? Or use scrap clay to make lots of tiny sprinkles? The possibilities are endless!

YIELD: 1 CUPCAKE

INGREDIENTS

CAKE:

³/₈" (1.6 cm) ball burnt umber

FROSTING:

¹/₈" (3.2 mm) ball cadmium red clay

¹/₄" (6.4 mm) ball white clay

CHERRY:

¹/₁₆" (1.6 mm) ball cadmium red clay

Needle or stippling tool

Headpin

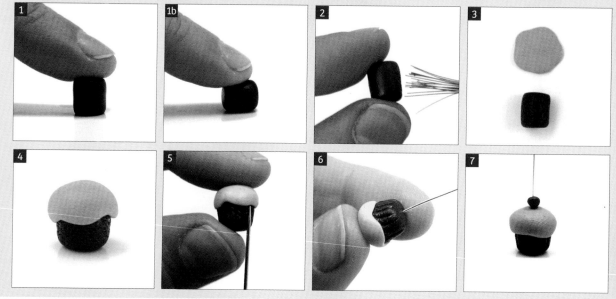

1. Start with the cake part. Roll the ball of brown clay into a small cylinder. Then set the cylinder on end and gently press to flatten the bottom and top.

2. Use a needle or stippling tool to make tiny indentations all over the surface. Don't forget the bottom!

3. Thoroughly mix the larger ball of red and the white clays to create an even pink color. Flatten the pink ball into an uneven pancake about twice the diameter of the top of your cake cylinder. The edge of the pancake should be a bit thinner than the middle.

4. Center the frosting on top of the cake, then gently fold down the edges of the frosting onto the cylinder.

5. Press the edge of a safety pin into the side of the cupcake to create parallel, evenly spaced lines all around.

6. Push the headpin through the center of your cupcake until the head is flush with the bottom.

7. Roll the remaining red clay into a very smooth ball. Slide the cherry onto the headpin and down until it rests on top. Bake for 18 minutes at 275° F (135° C).

. . . .
To Make a Cupcake Charm
. . . .

1. Finish the headpin in the cupcake into a closed, wrapped loop (see page 35).

2. Add the charm to a cell phone lariat.

Raspberry Chocolate Cupcakes

YIELD: 18 CUPCAKES

These richly chocolate cupcakes are balanced by the sweet tartness of raspberry frosting and are perfect for birthdays, dinner parties, or those afternoons when you just need a chocolate treat.

INGREDIENTS

4 tablespoons (60 ml) unsalted butter

¾ cup (180 ml) cocoa powder

1 cup (240 ml) hot water

2 (500 ml) cups sugar

1 teaspoon (5 ml) salt

1 teaspoon (5 ml) vanilla

2 eggs

2 cups (500 ml) unbleached flour

½ teaspoon (2.5 ml) baking powder

1¼ cup (300 ml) baking soda

¾ cup (180 ml) sour cream

DIRECTIONS: Preheat the oven to 350° F (175° C). Melt the butter over a double boiler. Gradually add the cocoa and small amounts of the hot water to the melted butter, and thoroughly blend into a smooth chocolate mixture. Pour the chocolate mixture into a mixing bowl, and whip in the sugar, salt, and vanilla. Mix in the eggs. Add half of the flour, along with the baking powder and soda. Mix in half of the sour cream. Add the remaining flour and sour cream, and mix until smooth. Fill the cupcake wrappers until they are about ⅔ full. Bake for 15 minutes, or until a toothpick comes out clean. Let the cupcakes cool, then frost them with the raspberry frosting and garnish with a fresh raspberry.

Raspberry Frosting

INGREDIENTS

⅙ cup (42 ml) seedless raspberry jam

1 tablespoon (15 ml) butter

1 cup (240 ml) semisweet chocolate chips

¼ cup (60 ml) sour cream

⅔ cup (160 ml) powdered sugar

DIRECTIONS: Over a double boiler, melt the jam and butter together. Add in the chocolate chips, and stir in until melted together. Remove from the heat. Stir in the sour cream and powdered sugar, and beat until smooth and thick.

Salty Soft Pretzel

SUSAN ✳ As a dedicated baseball fan, a salty jumbo soft pretzel is a major component of my ballpark routine—it keeps me cheering through the seventh-inning stretch. Often caked with a massive amount of sea salt, the pretzels are also fun to dust off to just the right amount of sodium while waiting through pitching changes, the superfluous salt joining the piles of peanut shells already lining the stands.

Miniature pretzels are sculpted just like real ones; the twist of the dough is identical. This recipe also teaches a different way to add pigment.

YIELD: 1 PRETZEL

INGREDIENTS

PRETZEL:

3/16" (4.7 mm) ball cadmium yellow clay

1/4" (6.4 mm) ball ecru clay

SALT:

1/16" (1.6 mm) ball white clay

Brown-orange oil pastel

Paintbrush

Tissue blade or utility knife

Safety pin or straight pin

Headpin

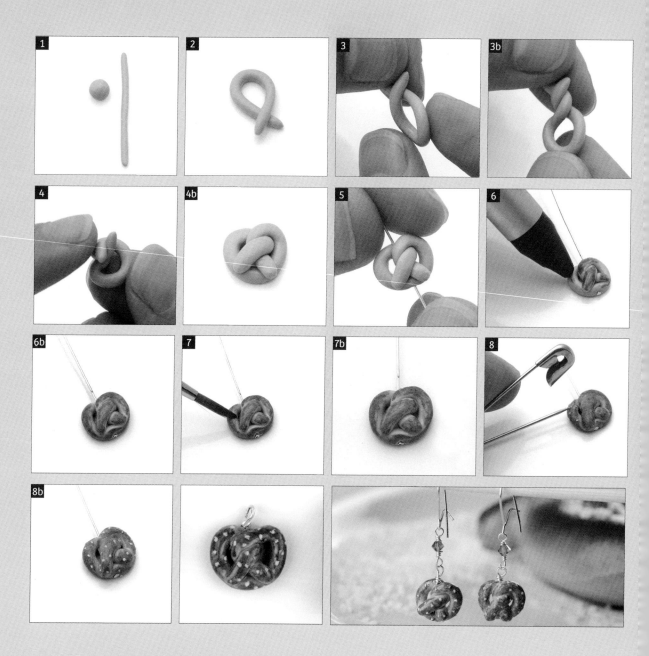

1. Thoroughly mix the ecru and yellow clays to create a warm beige. Roll the ball into a snake 2" (5 cm) long and about $1/8$" (3.2 mm) wide. The snake should be evenly thick so the pretzel doesn't turn out lopsided.

2. Form the snake into a crisscrossed loop, as shown.

3. Hold the crossed ends stationary between your thumb and forefinger and twist the bottom loop 180 degrees with your other hand.

4. Fold the twisted portion onto the loop side to create a pretzel shape. Align the crossed section in the center of the loop with the ends touching the edge of the pretzel.

5. Slide a headpin through the bottom, up through the twist, and out at the top (center). Be gentle to avoid pushing the bottom portion of the pretzel into the twist.

6. Rub some orange-brown oil pastel onto the pretzel. The color will look a little rough, but should evenly cover most of the surface except for the creases and joints.

7. With a clean paintbrush, gently brush the rough color to smooth it out, but avoid brushing into the creases. Your pretzel should look evenly toasted, but with the inner creases and joints still light and yellow. If you brush too hard and take off too much pigment, reapply the oil pastel and brush again. Wash your hands, the paintbrush, and your tile before moving on.

8. Roll the white clay into a thin, long snake, and cut it into teensy-tiny pieces with a tissue blade or a utility knife. Use a pin to press the small pieces onto your pretzel one at a time until it is adequately salted.

9. Bake for 15 minutes at 275° F (135° C).

. . . .
To Make Pretzel Earrings
. . . .

1. Create two matching pretzels.

2. Finish the headpin in each pretzel into a closed, wrapped loop (see page 35).

3. Add a 4mm light topaz crystal accent onto a double-sided loop (see page 36) above each pretzel.

4. Finish the earrings on your ear wires of choice. Your pretzels are now ready to supply some extra cheering power for your favorite team.

Swirly Lollipop

SUSAN ✳ This recipe is for one colorful, deliciously sweet lollipop, the kind enjoyed after a fun-filled day at the county fair, amusement park, or even the circus. I remember how, as a kid, these huge lollipops seemed nearly as big as my head.

At just about ¾" (19 mm) tall, this charm fits comfortably on a necklace. Our version features the full spectrum of color, in proper ROYGBIV order (well, almost—sorry indigo), but feel free to create your own color combination. You can even make the lollipop more authentic by mixing each color with an equal amount of translucent clay to make it look more like candy.

YIELD: 1 LOLLIPOP

INGREDIENTS

LOLLIPOP:

- Less than $1/8$" (3.2 mm) ball cadmium red clay
- Less than $1/8$" (3.2 mm) ball orange clay
- Less than $1/8$" (3.2 mm) ball cadmium yellow clay
- Less than $1/8$" (3.2 mm) ball green clay
- Less than $1/8$" (3.2 mm) ball cobalt blue clay
- Less than $1/8$" (3.2 mm) ball purple clay
- $1/4$" (6.4 mm) ball white clay

STICK:

- $1/8$" (3.2 mm) ball ecru clay
- Headpin

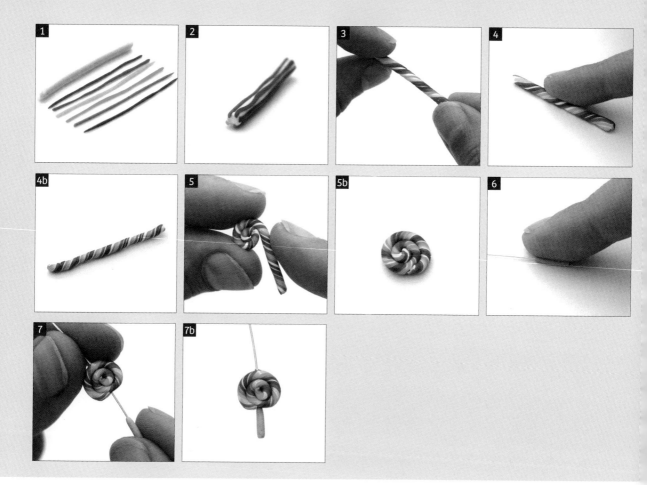

1. Roll the ball of white clay into a snake roughly 1" (2.5 cm) long. Roll each of the remaining colors, except for the ecru, into a thin snake of the same length.

2. Align the six color snakes in rainbow order around the outside of the white snake. Gently press each color snake into the white so it remains in place but is still raised above the center cane. Leave a bit of white space between each color snake, and keep the snakes as evenly spaced as possible.

3. Hold both ends of the snake in your hands and gently twist into a spiral.

4. Following the direction of the twist, roll the snake against your work surface until the rainbow is flattened and fully bonded to the white. The final smooth snake will be roughly 1½" (3.8 cm) long and less than ⅛" (3.2 mm) in diameter.

5. Lightly pinch one end of the snake and roll into a flat coil beginning with the pinched end. Continue coiling until you reach the end. Flatten the final end against the bottom of the coil with the back of your fingernail.

6. Roll the ecru clay into a snake, then slide it over the end of your headpin. Roll the clay against your work surface until you have a smooth cylinder fixed firmly around the headpin that is about ½" (1.3 cm) tall.

7. Slide the lollipop coil onto the headpin, passing the pin through the center of the coil, as shown, until it is pushing slightly into the ecru cylinder.

8. Bake for 15 minutes at 275° F (135° C).

To Make a Lollipop Necklace

1. Finish the headpin in the lollipop into a closed, wrapped loop (see page 35).

2. Add a jump ring or spring ring onto the wrapped loop.

3. String a necklace with rainbow-colored size 11 seed beads, then attach your lollipop.

Ice Cream Cone Delight

JESSICA ✻ I have always loved wandering into little local ice cream parlors, the air rich with the caramel crispness of fresh-baked waffle cones, colorful frosted tubs filled with wildly inventive flavors, and hand-written labels gently askew on the glass. Normally, I jealously guard my desserts against anyone who wants "just a taste," but I happily trade spoonfuls of ice cream with friends so that we can all sample a bunch of flavors.

We make this ice cream cone charm much like the real thing, baking the cone first to preserve its delicate texture. The best part about this recipe? We use a blunt #2 pencil as the mold for the cone—finally, they're useful for something better than test-taking!

YIELD: 1 CONE

INGREDIENTS

CONE:

¼" (6.4 mm) ball ecru clay

SCOOP:

¹⁄₁₆" (1.6 mm) ball raw sienna clay

³⁄₁₆" (9.5 mm) ball translucent clay

¼" (6.4 mm) ball white clay

Raw sienna soft pastel

Liquid clay

Blunt #2 pencil

Tool with a waffle-patterned handle,
   such as a stripping tool

Paintbrush

Headpin

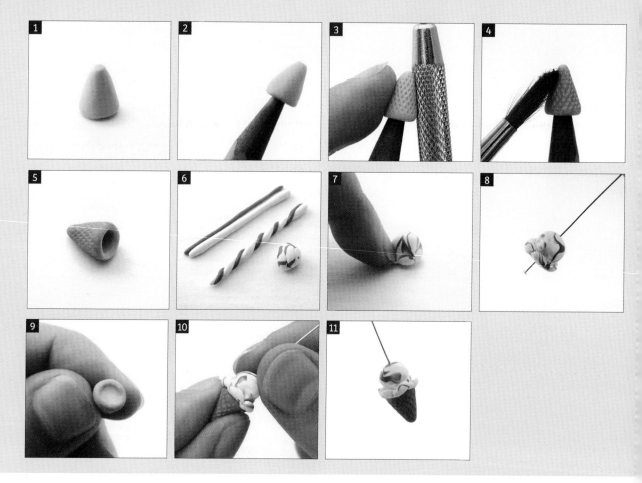

1. Roll the ecru clay into a smooth ball, then form it into a cone shape.

2. Press the cone over the tip of the blunt pencil to form a hollow cone. Note: It is easier to create the cone when your clay is cool. If your clay tends to get warm as you work with it, allow time between each of the cone steps for it to cool.

3. Use the textured side of a stippling tool to create an embossed diamond pattern on the outside of the cone. If the cone becomes distorted, use the back of your fingernail to coax the top edges of the cone back into an even shape.

4. Rub the raw sienna pastel against a scrap piece of paper until a small pile of powder forms. With a paintbrush, dab on a thin layer of powder to give the cone a toasty look. Hold your cone very gently, and twist to remove from the end of your pencil.

5. Bake the cone for 10 minutes at 275° F (135° C). Don't quench it at this point, since you want to keep the inside of your cone dry for the remainder of the project.

6. To create caramel ice cream, first mix the translucent and raw sienna clays. Marble the caramel with the white clay to create a sphere of vanilla-caramel swirl (see page 21).

7. Flatten the bottom edge of the marbled ball, then gently indent tiny half-moon shapes around the bottom edge using the end of your fingernail. Make sure your fingernail does not go all the way through the edge of the scoop.

8. Slide a headpin through the bottom of the scoop, leaving a small part of the head end exposed underneath the scoop.

9. Add a small amount of liquid clay to the inside of the baked cone, until the liquid is just shy of the top edge.

10. Attach the scoop to the top of the cone. Push the headpin down until you feel it touch the bottom of the inside of the cone.

11. To make the ice cream cone more secure (and realistic), pull down some of the edge of the scoop onto the side of the cone, and smooth away any tiny amounts of liquid clay that may have seeped out between the scoop and the cone.

12. Bake for 15 minutes at 275° F (135° C).

. . . .
To Make an Ice Cream Cone Charm Bracelet
. . . .

1. Make five different flavors of ice cream cones.

2. Finish the headpin in each cone into a closed, wrapped loop (see page 35).

3. String the ice cream cones on a bracelet with pale yellow size 11 seed beads.

A Shop Full of Flavors!

Everyone has a favorite ice cream flavor! Here are some variations to help you create a whole shop full of cones.

ORANGE SORBET = $^1/_8$" (3.2 mm) ball orange + $^1/_4$" (6.4 mm) ball translucent clays

Mix thoroughly for a uniform color.

CHOCOLATE = $^1/_8$" (3.2 mm) ball brown + $^1/_4$" (6.4 mm) ball translucent clays

Mix thoroughly for a uniform color.

STRAWBERRY SWIRL = Two $^1/_{16}$" (1.6 mm) balls cadmium red + $^1/_4$" (6.4 mm) ball white + $^1/_8$" (3.2 mm) ball translucent clays

Thoroughly mix one cadmium red ball with the white to create a creamy pink. Mix the other cadmium red ball with the translucent to create a dark strawberry jam color. Marble these two together (see page 21).

CHOCOLATE CHIP = $^1/_4$" (6.4 mm) ball burnt sienna + $^1/_4$" (6.4 mm) ball white clays

Roll the burnt sienna into a flat sheet, then finely dice it to create chocolate chips. Bake the chips at the same time as your cone. Mix the baked chips into the white for chocolate chip ice cream.

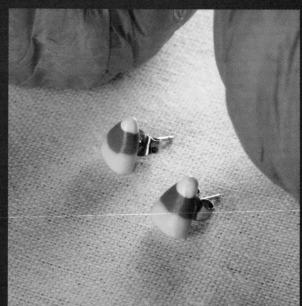

7

Holiday Goodies

No holiday or celebration is complete without a special food. What would Valentine's Day be like without conversation hearts, or Halloween without candy corn? From warm pumpkin pie at the end of a Thanksgiving meal to decorating holiday cookies for friends and relatives, special treats such as these remind us of cherished times spent with family and friends.

Valentine's Day Conversation Hearts

SUSAN ✳ Whether or not you celebrate Valentine's Day, it's hard to avoid these brightly colored candies in February. I feel as if I've made it incredibly clear to everyone I know that I can't stand the taste of these things, but a box or two inevitably appears on my desk from festive colleagues. Even though the actual candies seem inedible to me, there is something about food that talks that I just can't resist, whether traditional and sweet ("be mine") or oddly tech-savvy ("email me").

This recipe uses the phrase "kiss me" since it is both traditional and symmetrical, and therefore easier for beginning writers. Once you've got the writing down, feel free to personalize these charms for your friends, family, and, of course, those persistent colleagues (or classmates).

YIELD: 1 HEART

INGREDIENTS

¹/₈" (3.2 mm) ball magenta clay

³/₁₆" (4.7 mm) ball cadmium red clay

³/₈" (9.5 mm) ball white clay

Figure-eight loop (see page 37)

Utility knife

Safety pin

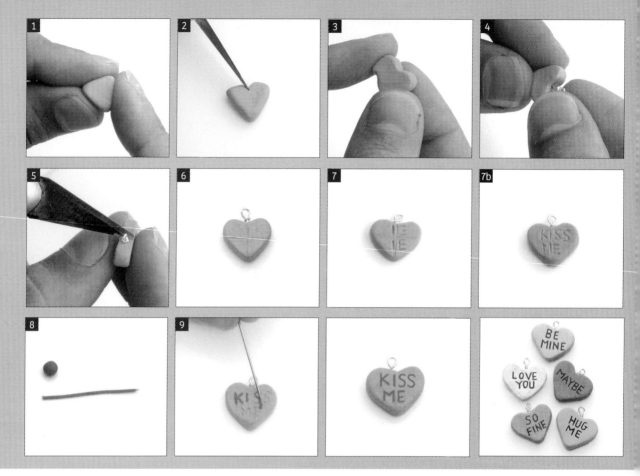

1. Thoroughly mix the white and red clays. Flatten the ball into a ⅛"-(3.2 mm-) thick pancake, then pinch the clay to create a triangle.

2. Make a small cut in the center of one side with your utility knife, then push each side of the cut outward.

3. Smooth each side by pulling the inside of the cut outward onto the side of the triangle.

4. Create a small incision with your utility knife in the notch at the top of the heart, then insert the figure-eight pin. Gently press the heart to fix the pin in place and close the incision.

5. Using the back edge of a utility knife, smooth any

remaining roughness around the figure-eight pin.

6. Before you start writing, create guidelines. Use a safety pin to make two faint lines: one marking the vertical middle, the other the horizontal middle.

7. Use your safety pin to imprint the letters from the center outward. Space your letters evenly.

8. To fill in the text with color, roll the magenta clay into a thin snake, roughly as wide as the pin imprint.

9. Cut the thin snake into short segments, and guide each segment into the letter impressions.

10. Smooth out the finished written surface by pressing the heart gently against your work surface.

11. Bake for 15 minutes at 275° F (135° C). Leave the baked heart unglazed to keep the chalky quality of the candy.

To Make a Candy Heart Bracelet

1. Create six hearts, one in each color. Wrap a 3mm opaque pink accent bead above each heart, and leave the top loop open (see page 36).

2. Individually attach each charm onto a silver bracelet chain, spacing each charm so there is just less than 1" (2.5 cm) between each heart for a 7" (17.8 cm) bracelet.

The Many Colors of Love

Although their flavor never changes, conversation hearts traditionally come in six pastel colors: pink, white, violet, yellow, orange, and green. The mixing directions below cover every flavor in the box.

WHITE: $3/8$" (9.5 mm) ball white clay

ORANGE: $1/4$" (6.4 mm) ball orange + $5/16$" (8 mm) ball white clay

GREEN: $3/16$" (4.7 mm) ball cadmium yellow + $1/8$" (3.2 mm) ball green + $5/16$" (8 mm) ball white clays

YELLOW: $1/4$" (6.4 mm) ball cadmium yellow + $1/4$" (6.4 mm) ball white clays

PURPLE: $3/16$" (4.7 mm) ball purple + $1/8$" (3.2 mm) ball cadmium red + $1/4$" (6.4 mm) ball white clays

For even more variety, try other popular phrases: "love you," "hug me," "be mine," "so fine," and "maybe." You can also create your own messages, but be prepared to break out the texting skills; any word should be five letters or less to fit, and for authenticity be written in all capital letters.

Halloween Candy Corn

JESSICA ✳ Every year, the first appearance of candy corn in the grocery store signals the true beginning of fall, which means it's time to start seriously planning our Halloween costumes. My personal favorite from childhood was the year I was a superhero, complete with shiny handmade cape and nifty boots. Of course, I kept having to tell people that, no, I was not Superman; I was Super Jessie.

For this project we'll create a piece of candy corn a bit smaller than the real kind.

YIELD: 1 PIECE

INGREDIENTS

⅛" (3.2 mm) ball white clay

³/₁₆" (4.7 mm) ball orange clay

¼" (6.4 mm) cadmium yellow clay

2 ear posts with 4mm flat pads

Cyanoacrylate glue

Needle tool

Sandpaper (220 grit)

Cotton swab

Rubbing alcohol

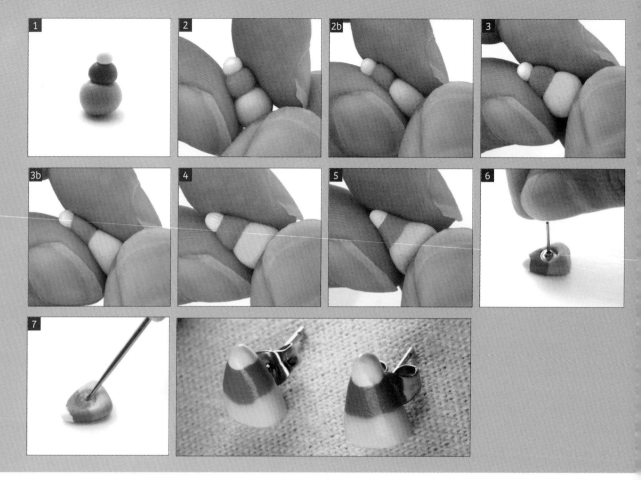

1. Start with nice warm clay. Not sticky or mushy, but warm, so the three layers of color will bind together. Start by stacking very smooth balls of the white, orange, and yellow clays, making a snowman shape.

2. Holding the stack as shown, gently press it half-way flat. You don't want it completely squished, just gently flattened.

3. Rotate the flattened corn 90 degrees in your fingers. It should look a little bit more like candy corn now—the rounded edges of your spheres of clay should be flattened a bit and starting to merge into the next layer of color. Flatten the corn again, just as you did before.

4. Turn it another 90 degrees. Your corn should look even smoother and the layers more fused together.

5. Keep repeating the flattening and turning until your corn is completely smooth and the layers are nicely bound together. The edges should be slightly rounded. Don't worry if the layers aren't completely straight and even—real candy corn isn't perfectly straight and even either!

6. Decide which side of your candy corn is your favorite, and place it facedown on your baking tile. This side will be the front of your earrings. If you have fingerprints on the surface, don't worry—they will be mostly eliminated when you press the flat pad of your ear post into the back of the corn to create an indentation

7. Remove the ear post, then use a needle tool to create a rough surface inside the indentation. This creates more surface area for the glue to bond, making for stronger earrings.

8. Bake for 15 minutes at 275° F (135° C).

To Make Candy Corn Stud Earrings

1. Make two matching candy corns.

2. Rub the front of each earring post pad over sandpaper to rough it up.

3. Rub the indentation in the back of each candy corn and the pad of each ear post with a cotton swab dipped in rubbing alcohol to remove any residual surface oils and metal flecks.

4. Add a drop of cyanoacrylate glue to the front of each ear post pad, then press the pad into the indentation in the candy corn. Wipe off any extra glue using a toothpick (not your fingers!). Let set overnight, or for at least 6 hours.

5. If you'd like to glaze the candy corn, glaze them after they have been glued onto the posts.

Thanksgiving Pumpkin Pie

JESSICA ✳ Thanksgiving just wouldn't be complete without pumpkin pie! It never matters how much turkey, garlic mashed potatoes, nutty mushroom vegetarian loafy thing, or salad, green beans, and other dishes we eat: we all always still have room for pie. That's why we always make at least two pumpkin pies at Thanksgiving, and why this recipe makes eight charms—perfect for a necklace, charm bracelet, or individual gifts. The whipped cream is optional, of course.

YIELD: 8 SLICES

INGREDIENTS

CRUST:
³/₈" (9.5 mm) ball ecru clay
³/₁₆" (4.7 mm) ball ecru clay

FILLING:
⅝" (15.9 mm) ball orange clay

WHIPPED CREAM:
³/₈" (9.5 mm) ball white clay

Liquid clay
Ground allspice
Raw sienna soft pastel
Large double-ball stylus or needle tool
Paintbrush
Tissue blade or razor blade
8 figure-eight loops (see page 37)

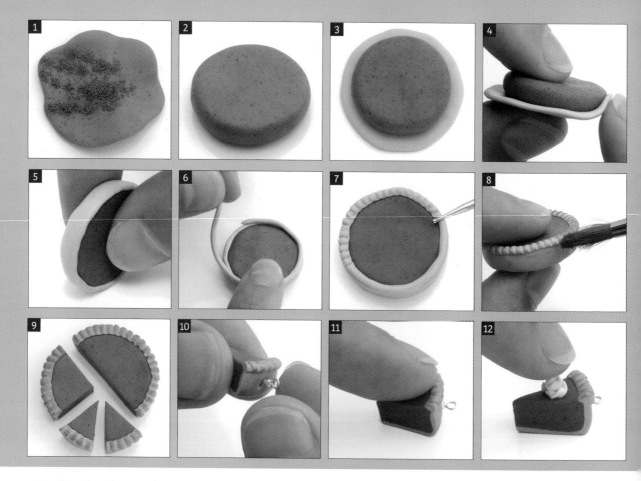

1. We'll make this pie from the inside out, starting with the filling. Thoroughly mix the orange clay with a big pinch of allspice. It's easiest if you first flatten the clay, then roll it with the allspice into a log and flatten it again. Keep working the clay; the spice will eventually mix in to make your orange a bit darker.

2. Roll the spicy orange clay into a smooth ball, then flatten it into a thick pancake about the size of two stacked quarters. Make sure it's flat and even on top; you don't want a bowl in the middle. Wash your hands and tile to remove any orange.

3. Roll the larger ball of ecru clay into a smooth ball, then flatten it into an even, thin pancake about $3/16$" (4.7 mm) larger than the filling on all sides. Place the filling in the middle of the flat crust, pressing the center to remove any air bubbles between the filling and crust.

4. Gently fold up the edges of the crust until they are even with the top of the pie filling.

5. Roll the pie like a wheel to smooth and flatten the side, as well as to bind the crust to the filling.

6. Roll the smaller ball of ecru clay into a narrow snake the same length as the circumference of the pie crust. Add it around the top of the pie.

7. Use the side of a stylus or needle tool to make evenly spaced indentations all around the edge of the crust.

8. Rub the raw sienna pastel against a scrap piece of paper until a small pile of powder forms. Dip your paintbrush in the powder and dab on a browned, baked look all over the crust. It doesn't need to be completely even—in fact, it will look more realistic if it isn't. Wash your hands, the paintbrush, and your tile before moving on.

9. Slice the pie in half with a tissue blade, then into quarters, and then into eighths.

10. Insert a figure-eight loop into each slice. Insert the loop vertically until the bottom loop is entirely within

Whip Up Some Whipped Cream

Whipped cream is easiest to make when the clay is a bit stiff.

1. Roll out a thin log of white clay, about 1" (2.54 cm) long. Flatten the log in your hands (not on your tile).

2. Pinch either end of the flattened log and twist to create a spiral.

3. Starting with one end, coil the spiral into a puff of whipped cream. You'll probably need to repeat these steps from the beginning for each dollop of whipped cream, since the spiral quickly gets stretched out and deformed.

the clay, then twist it 90 degrees until it is horizontal.

11. Press down on the filling to secure the loop in place.

12. Make a puff of whipped cream (see sidebar on previous page). Add a drop of liquid clay to the underside of the whipped cream and gently press it into place.

13. Bake for 15 minutes at 275° F (135° C).

. . . .

To Make a Pumpkin Pie Necklace

. . . .

1. Wrap a 4mm copper accent bead above each of the eight pie wedges, and close off the top loops (see page 37).

2. String the pies onto beading wire or braided nylon with copper-lined size 11 seed beads.

Sugar Cookies

YIELD: APPROXIMATELY 24 COOKIES

These holiday classics are enjoyed every year by our family at Christmas. We also enjoy them on other holidays by popular request when we have the energy to decorate them. We typically add the sugary decorations before baking, but these cookies can be quite delicious frosted as well.

INGREDIENTS

1½ cups (360 ml) confectioners' sugar

1 cup (240 ml) butter, softened

1 egg

1 teaspoon (5 ml) vanilla

½ teaspoon (2.5 ml) almond flavoring

2½ (600 ml) cups all purpose flour

1 teaspoon (5 ml) baking soda

1 teaspoon (5 ml) cream of tartar

DIRECTIONS: Mix together the sugar and butter thoroughly. Add in the eggs and flavorings; mix thoroughly. Gradually stir in the dry ingredients, forming a soft dough. Gather the dough into a ball and refrigerate for at least 2 hours. Once the dough has firmed, divide in half. Preheat the oven to 375° F (190° C). On a lightly floured surface, roll out each half of the dough to 3/16" (4.7 mm) thick. Using a variety of seasonal cookie cutter shapes, cut out as many cookies as possible, and roll out the dough again until none is left. Place the cookie shapes onto an ungreased baking sheet. Decorate with the necessary sprinkles or other sugary decor, and then bake for 7 to 8 minutes or until the cookie edges are delicately golden brown. Cool for a few minutes before indulging in the holiday goodness.

Gingerbread People Cookies

SUSAN ✳ Holiday cookie baking in our family is an involved process. The creative cookie shapes and decorations are never simple or standard, and the most fun of all is morphing gingerbread men and women into members of the family. We add extra pieces of dough to make the correct hairstyle, use the right sprinkle color to match the eyes, and customize each outfit. They are indeed "sweeter" versions of ourselves.

This recipe makes one gingerbread cookie, complete with traditional icing. The allspice is used for its visual effect, but a wonderful bonus is its smell during the sculpting process, which will fill your home with warmth and festivity.

YIELD: 1 COOKIE

INGREDIENTS

COOKIE:

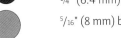

¼" (6.4 mm) ball burnt sienna clay

⁵/₁₆" (8 mm) ball tan clay

FROSTING:

¹/₁₆" (1.6 mm) ball white clay

Ground allspice (optional)

Figure-eight loop (page 37)

Straight pin

Utility knife

Needle tool

Scrap piece of heavy paper or cardstock

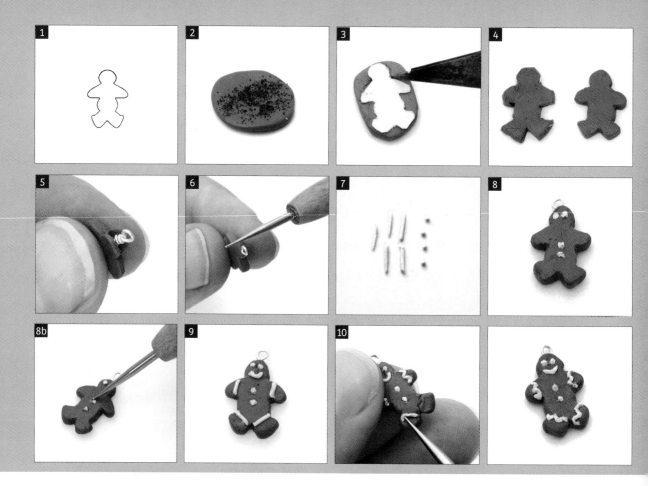

1. Trace the gingerbread man shape onto a scrap piece of heavy paper or cardstock. Cut out the figure as carefully as possible; this will be your template.

2. Thoroughly mix the brown and tan clays to form an even medium brown. Flatten the clay into a pancake, add the allspice, and mix thoroughly. The finished mix should have spice evenly suspended throughout.

3. Flatten the gingerbread mixture into a disk roughly ⅛" (3.2 mm) thick and slightly bigger than the cutout. Carefully flatten your gingerbread man template on the disk. Cut around the template with your utility knife, cutting outward from the torso where possible. Set aside the excess clay.

4. Remove the paper cutout. Your figure will probably be a little rough (as shown at left). Round and smooth out the rough edges with the back of your fingernail or the side of a needle tool (shown after smoothing at right).

5. Make a small cut into the head and insert the figure-eight pin. Press the cut back together to secure the pin in place.

6. Smooth the head with the side of a utility knife or needle tool to erase the cut lines. Wash your hands before moving on to the next step.

7. Roll the white clay into a snake roughly 2" (5.1 cm) long. Cut the snake into a total of nine pieces: four small balls (for the eyes and buttons), and five 1/8" (3.2 mm) lengths (for the smile and clothing).

8. Place the white segments onto your cookie, beginning with the eyes and buttons. Fix the pieces into place with the tip of a straight pin.

9. Curve one piece of white clay for the smile, then place the remaining four segments straight across the ends of the arms and legs for clothing.

10. To turn the straight lines of clothing into squiggles, use a straight pin to attach one end of the segment to the ginger clay. Lightly push the

segment up and down with the end of the pin until it is evenly squiggled. The finished icing should be firmly attached but slightly raised above the flattened cookie part.

11. Bake for 15 minutes at 275° F (135° C).

To Make Very Merry Earrings

1. Make two matching gingerbread charms.

2. Add three beads onto a double-sided loop (see page 36) above each cookie in the following order: a bright emerald green seed bead on the bottom, a red and green striped size 8 bead in the middle, and a red seed bead on top.

3. Finish the earrings on ear wires of your choice. We've attached our finished earrings onto closed-back sterling silver ear wires to keep the gingerbread men from running off our ears.

Variations

Why stop with gingerbread men? Create a whole bunch of different cookies and make yourself (or a friend) a holiday charm bracelet.

DIFFERENT SHAPES. To make a variety of gingerbread or sugar cookies, use the templates below.

SUGAR COOKIES. To create sugar cookie dough, mix a $5/16$" (8 mm) ball of ecru and a $3/16$" (4.7 mm) ball of yellow clays for each cookie.

ICING. To get the cookie-specific icing effect, mix your desired frosting color clay with translucent clay (about double the amount of colored clay). The finished baked charm will be mostly opaque, but with a frosty appearance resembling densely packed sugar frosting.

Resources

Here are a few of our favorite retailers and sources of information.

Polymer clay

You can find polymer clay and sculpting tools at nearly any local craft store. There are frequent sales, so keep an eye out for discounts. There are also places online where you can purchase clay and tools. One major caveat: do not purchase clay online during the warm months. There is a fairly high chance that your clay will cook in the back of the shipping truck en route, and there's nothing worse than unusable craft supplies! For similar reasons (unknown provenance), we caution against purchasing raw clay from sites such as ebay.

www.polymerclayexpress.com is a site we've purchased from. They have great prices, a comprehensive selection of clay and tools.

Jewelry-making

For basic jewelry-making supplies and beads, local craft stores are great. Specialty bead stores are better. But online sources will usually give you the best value for your dollar, as long as it's a reputable company. Here are a few that we like:

www.firemountaingems.com Definitely not the least expensive, but a great place to find findings, and even another kind of polymer clay: Kato Polyclay.

www.artbeads.com A small company with a carefully edited selection, but completely free shipping, even if you only purchase one pair of ear wires.

www.etsy.com A vast, incredible site filled with all manner of handmade goodies and supplies. A great place to get inspiration, as well as hard-to-find and custom-made findings.

Information and help

There are some great online sources of polymer clay information:

www.glassattic.com Encyclopedic and amazing.

www.polymerclaycentral.com Great forums where you can ask any question you might have about working with polymer clay!

www.craftster.org Another forum-based site where people share their projects (in all mediums!) and where you can ask specific questions.

Index